# THE PEGAN COOKBOOK

LOSE WEIGHT AND GET HEALTHY WITH RECIPES BASED ON FRESH FRUITS, VEGETABLES, AND HEALTHY FATS. CREATE YOUR MEAL PLAN EASILY AND ENJOY BECOMING THE BEST VERSION OF YOURSELF.

Susan Reddis

© COPYRIGHT 2021 - ALL RIGHTS RESERVED.

THIS DOCUMENT IS GEARED TOWARDS PROVIDING EXACT AND RELIABLE INFORMATION IN REGARD TO THE TOPIC AND ISSUE COVERED. THE PUBLICATION IS SOLD WITH THE IDEA THAT THE PUBLISHER IS NOT REQUIRED TO RENDER ACCOUNTING, OFFICIALLY PERMITTED, OR OTHERWISE, QUALIFIED SERVICES. IF ADVICE IS NECESSARY, LEGAL OR PROFESSIONAL, A PRACTICED INDIVIDUAL IN THE PROFESSION SHOULD BE ORDERED.

- FROM A DECLARATION OF PRINCIPLES WHICH WAS ACCEPTED AND APPROVED EQUALLY BY A COMMITTEE OF THE AMERICAN BAR ASSOCIATION AND A COMMITTEE OF PUBLISHERS AND ASSOCIATIONS.

IN NO WAY IS IT LEGAL TO REPRODUCE, DUPLICATE, OR TRANSMIT ANY PART OF THIS DOCUMENT IN EITHER ELECTRONIC MEANS OR IN PRINTED FORMAT. RECORDING OF THIS PUBLICATION IS STRICTLY PROHIBITED, AND ANY STORAGE OF THIS DOCUMENT IS NOT ALLOWED UNLESS WITH WRITTEN PERMISSION FROM THE PUBLISHER. ALL RIGHTS RESERVED.

THE INFORMATION PROVIDED HEREIN IS STATED TO BE TRUTHFUL AND CONSISTENT, IN THAT ANY LIABILITY, IN TERMS OF INATTENTION OR OTHERWISE, BY ANY USAGE OR ABUSE OF ANY POLICIES, PROCESSES, OR DIRECTIONS CONTAINED WITHIN IS THE SOLITARY AND UTTER RESPONSIBILITY OF THE RECIPIENT READER. UNDER NO CIRCUMSTANCES WILL ANY LEGAL RESPONSIBILITY OR BLAME BE HELD AGAINST THE PUBLISHER FOR ANY REPARATION, DAMAGES, OR MONETARY LOSS DUE TO THE INFORMATION HEREIN, EITHER DIRECTLY OR INDIRECTLY.

RESPECTIVE AUTHORS OWN ALL COPYRIGHTS NOT HELD BY THE PUBLISHER.

THE INFORMATION HEREIN IS OFFERED FOR INFORMATIONAL PURPOSES SOLELY AND IS UNIVERSAL AS SO. THE PRESENTATION OF THE INFORMATION IS WITHOUT A CONTRACT OR ANY TYPE OF GUARANTEE ASSURANCE.

THE TRADEMARKS THAT ARE USED ARE WITHOUT ANY CONSENT, AND THE PUBLICATION OF THE TRADEMARK IS WITHOUT PERMISSION OR BACKING BY THE TRADEMARK OWNER. ALL TRADEMARKS AND BRANDS WITHIN THIS BOOK ARE FOR CLARIFYING PURPOSES ONLY AND ARE OWNED BY THE OWNERS THEMSELVES, NOT AFFILIATED WITH THIS DOCUMENT.

# TABLE OF CONTENTS

**INTRODUCTION**   7

**CHAPTER 1: UNDERSTANDING THE PEGAN DIET**   8

- 1.1 WHAT IS PEGAN DIET?   8
- 1.2 FOODS TO CONSUME AND AVOID   8
- 1.3 ADVANTAGES AND DISADVANTAGES OF PEGAN DIET   9
- 1.4 7 DAY MEAL PLAN   9
- DAY 1   10
- DAY 2   10
- DAY 3   10
- DAY 4   10
- DAY 5   10
- DAY 6   11
- DAY 7   11

**CHAPTER 2: EASY BREAKFAST RECIPES**   13

1. CRISPY HASH BROWN HAYSTACKS   14
2. DARK CHOCOLATE QUINOA BREAKFAST BOWL   14
3. BUCKWHEAT CREPES   15
4. PEANUT BUTTER & JELLY CHIA PUDDING   15
5. RAW-NOLA   16
6. ROASTED SWEET POTATO & KALE BREAKFAST HASH   16
7. SAVORY BREAKFAST SALAD   17
8. CHOCOLATE CHIP OATMEAL COOKIE PANCAKE   18
9. DARK CHOCOLATE GRANOLA   18
10. ROASTED RAINBOW VEGETABLE BOWL   19
11. BANANA WALNUT PANCAKES   19
12. SPICY TEMPEH BREAKFAST SAUSAGE   20
13. CRISPY EGGPLANT BACON   21
14. CANDIED ORANGE PEEL GRANOLA   21
15. CRUNCHY ALMOND GRANOLA   22
16. FARRO-AND-TOMATO SALAD WITH CRISPY CAPERS   22
17. PEANUT BUTTER BANANA BREAD GRANOLA   23
18. GRAB AND GO CRANBERRY GRANOLA BARS   23
19. STEAMED WILD RICE WITH TOASTED HAZELNUT BUTTER   24
20. MAPLE-CITRUS SALAD WITH COCONUT   24
21. QUICK TANGELO MARMALADE   24
22. SWEET POTATO BREAKFAST BOWL   25
23. VEGAN GINGER BREAD SCONES WITH VANILLA BEAN GLAZE   25
24. PECAN PIE OVERNIGHT OATS   26
25. GINGER CORIANDER SPROUTED LENTILS AVOCADO TOAST   26
26. SLOW COOKER STEEL CUT OATS WITH APPLE & CRANBERRIES   27
27. STRAWBERRY BALSAMIC JAM   27
28. VEGAN FRENCH TOAST   28
29. WHOLE WHEAT VEGAN WAFFLES   28
30. PUMPKIN PANCAKES   29
31. CARROT WAFFLES   29
32. TOFU SCRAMBLE   29
33. AVOCADO TOAST   30
34. VEGAN CARROT LOX   30
35. OATMEAL BREAKFAST COOKIES   31
36. MANGO COCONUT MUFFINS   31
37. VEGAN SCONES WITH RASPBERRIES   32
38. OVERNIGHT OATS   32
39. CINNAMON PECAN MUESLI   33

40. NUT BUTTER TOAST — 33
41. BANANA BAKED OATMEAL — 34
42. ACAI BOWL — 34
43. VEGAN BLUEBERRY PANCAKES — 35
44. APPLE CINNAMON STEEL CUT OATS — 35
45. ORANGE & MINT SALAD — 36
46. PISTACHIO & CARDAMOM BUTTER — 36
47. THREE-GRAIN PORRIDGE — 36
48. VEGAN BANANA & WALNUT BREAD — 36
49. BLACKCURRANT COMPOTE — 37
50. BREAKFAST NAAN — 37
51. PEANUT BUTTER & BANANA OVERNIGHT OATS — 37
52. EASY CANNED PEACHES — 38
53. FLAXSEED BLUEBERRY OATMEAL — 39
54. CHIA PEANUT BUTTER OATS — 39
55. SCRAMBLED TOFU BREAKFAST BURRITO — 39
56. SEEDY HUMMUS TOAST — 40
57. GREEK CHICKPEAS ON TOAST — 40
58. ALMOND MILK & CHAI QUINOA BOWL — 41
59. SPICY SCRAMBLED TOFU BREAKFAST TACOS — 41
60. FLUFFY VEGAN PROTEIN PANCAKES — 42
61. SIMPLE VEGAN OMELET — 42
62. CINNAMON ROLL OVERNIGHT OATS — 43
63. EVERYTHING BAGEL AVOCADO TOAST — 43
64. QUICK-COOKING OATS — 43
65. PEANUT BUTTER BANANA CINNAMON TOAST — 44
66. WHITE BEAN & AVOCADO TOAST — 44
67. VEGAN PUMPKIN BREAD — 44
68. OLD-FASHIONED OATMEAL — 45
69. APPLE CINNAMON OVERNIGHT OATS — 45
70. BLUEBERRY BANANA OVERNIGHT OATS — 45

## CHAPTER 3: VEGAN DRINKS AND SMOOTHIES — 47

1. BLACK CHERRY BOURBON COLA SMASH — 48
2. PINK DRINK — 48
3. GINGER BEER MOJITO — 48
4. FROZEN BLACKBERRY COOLERS — 49
5. STRAWBERRY PEACH ICED TEA — 49
6. FROZEN COCONUT MOJITO — 49
7. WATERMELON BASIL COOLER — 50
8. CUCUMBER VODKA SODA — 50
9. SUMMER BERRY SANGRIA — 50
10. COCONUT MATCHA HORCHATA: MATCHATA — 51
11. ORANGE PEACH MANGO SPRITZER — 51
12. ROSE, LEMON, STRAWBERRY INFUSED WATER — 52
13. SKINNY CHAMPAGNE MARGARITAS — 52
14. WATERMELON & CUCUMBER MOJITOS — 52
15. FROSTED LEMONADE — 53
16. ORANGE AND SPICE HOT CHOCOLATE — 53
17. LEMON GINGER DETOX TEA — 53
18. CARROT, PINEAPPLE & GINGER JUICE — 54
19. BEST VEGAN CHOCOLATE MILKSHAKE — 54
20. VEGAN STRAWBERRY MILKSHAKE — 54
21. MIXED BERRY YOGURT SMOOTHIE — 55
22. CHOCOLATE ALMOND BUTTER SMOOTHIE/ SMOOTHIE BOWL — 55
23. CHOCOLATE CHERRY SMOOTHIE — 55
24. BANANA SPLIT SMOOTHIE — 56
25. MANGO PINEAPPLE SMOOTHIE — 56
26. FRESH GREEN HEMP SMOOTHIE — 56
27. BLUEBERRY BANANA SMOOTHIE — 57
28. FRUITY CHIA SEED SMOOTHIE — 57
29. HOT PINK BEET SMOOTHIE WITH CITRUS — 57

| | |
|---|---|
| 30. CHOCOLATE BANANA OAT BREAKFAST SMOOTHIE | 58 |
| 31. BERRY BEET VELVET SMOOTHIE | 58 |
| 32. SPICED STRAWBERRY & GOJI BERRY SMOOTHIE | 58 |
| 33. DEEP TROPICAL VIBES GREEN SMOOTHIE | 59 |
| 34. VEGAN PEANUT BUTTER MOCHA SMOOTHIE | 59 |
| 35. GINGER C & GREENS SMOOTHIE | 59 |
| 36. VEGAN PUMPKIN SMOOTHIE WITH GINGER & CARDAMOM | 60 |
| 37. BEET & BLOOD ORANGE SPICE SMOOTHIE | 60 |
| 38. GOLDEN PEACH SUNRISE SMOOTHIE | 60 |
| 39. KIWI FRUIT SMOOTHIE | 61 |
| 40. CREAMY MANGO & COCONUT SMOOTHIE | 61 |

## CHAPTER 4: VEGAN LUNCH RECIPES — 63

| | |
|---|---|
| 1. GRILLED CAULIFLOWER WEDGES | 64 |
| 2. SPICY EDAMAME | 64 |
| 3. GARBANZO-STUFFED MINI PEPPERS | 64 |
| 4. WAFFLE-IRON ACORN SQUASH | 65 |
| 5. MINTY PEAS & ONIONS | 65 |
| 6. CHILI-LIME ROASTED CHICKPEAS | 65 |
| 7. CABBAGE & RUTABAGA SLAW | 66 |
| 8. HOMEMADE POTATO CHIPS | 66 |
| 9. CRUNCHY BREADSTICKS | 66 |
| 10. WARM TASTY GREENS WITH GARLIC | 67 |
| 11. SWEET POTATO KIEV | 67 |
| 12. QUINOA, EDAMAME AND BROCCOLI SALAD | 68 |
| 13. VEGAN TOMATO TART | 68 |
| 14. STUFFED ROAST PUMPKIN | 69 |
| 15. QUINOA PILAF | 69 |
| 16. MUSHROOM CACCIATORE PASTA | 70 |
| 17. CREAMY PUMPKIN, SAGE & BROCCOLI SPELT PASTA BAKES | 70 |
| 18. CREAMY VEGAN SUN-DRIED TOMATO & BROCCOLINI GNOCCHI | 71 |
| 19. PASTA NOURISH BOWL | 71 |
| 20. SWEET POTATO NOODLES WITH CRISPY KALE | 72 |
| 21. CILANTRO POTATOES | 72 |
| 22. LEMON GARLIC MUSHROOMS | 72 |
| 23. ROASTED ASPARAGUS & LEEKS | 73 |
| 24. SPICY GRILLED EGGPLANT | 73 |
| 25. SIMPLE GUACAMOLE | 73 |
| 26. THYME SEA SALT CRACKERS | 74 |
| 27. THYME ZUCCHINI SAUTE' | 74 |
| 28. FRESH FRUIT BOWL | 74 |
| 29. GARLIC-CHIVE BAKED FRIES | 75 |
| 30. ROASTED RADISHES | 75 |
| 31. FAST FRUIT SALSA | 75 |
| 32. GARLIC-ROSEMARY BRUSSELS SPROUTS | 76 |
| 33. JICAMA CITRUS SALAD | 76 |
| 34. ROASTED BEET WEDGES | 76 |
| 35. SWEET POTATOES WITH KALE AND CARAMELIZED ONIONS | 77 |
| 36. BAKED GARLIC PEPPER POLENTA FRIES | 77 |
| 37. ARRABBIATA BEANS | 78 |
| 38. ROASTED CAULIFLOWER GARLIC HUMMUS | 78 |
| 39. BEST DRY SAUTED MUSHROOMS | 78 |
| 40. CASHEW CREAM CHEESE | 79 |
| 41. SEA SALT CHICKPEA CRACKERS | 79 |
| 42. RED LENTIL FLATBREAD PIZZA CRUST | 80 |
| 43. REFRIED BLACK BEANS | 80 |
| 44. BETTER THAN TRADER JOE'S CAULIFLOWER GNOCCHI | 81 |
| 45. ARROZ VERDE - MEXICAN GREEN RICE | 81 |
| 46. NON-CREAMY POTATO SALAD | 82 |
| 47. TIKKA MASALA WITH ROASTED VEGETABLES | 82 |
| 48. CHICKPEA FAJITAS | 83 |
| 49. CURRIED CAULIFLOWER SOUP | 83 |

| | |
|---|---|
| 50. INSTANT POT CILANTRO LIME BLACK BEANS | 84 |
| 51. QUINOA FLATBREAD PIZZA CRUST | 84 |
| 52. EASY PEA SOUP | 85 |
| 53. GLUTEN-FREE TORTILLAS | 85 |
| 54. CHEESY OIL-FREE KALE CHIPS | 86 |
| 55. PUMPKIN LENTIL SOUP WITH GINGER | 86 |
| 56. INSTANT POT GARLIC RICE | 87 |
| 57. CHICKPEA FLOUR PANCAKE-FENNEL & OLIVE | 87 |
| 58. SMOOCHING MUSHROOMS ON TOP | 88 |
| 59. POTATO STUFFED PEPPERS | 88 |
| 60. SMOKED TOFU & HUMMUS BUDDHA BOWL | 89 |
| 61. VEGAN ZUCCHINI CORN FRITTERS | 89 |
| 62. LENTIL BEAN SALAD | 90 |
| 63. SPEEDY VEGAN BURRITO | 91 |
| 64. VEGAN CHEESE SAVOURY SANDWICH FILLING | 91 |
| 65. RAUNCHY SWEET POTATO SALAD | 91 |
| 66. VEGETABLE HERB PASTA SALAD | 92 |
| 67. CRISPY BUFFALO TOFU WRAP | 92 |
| 68. TEMPEH SANDWICH | 93 |
| 69. AUBERGINE CURRY - EGGPLANT CURRY | 94 |
| 70. PERUVIAN SANDWICH | 94 |

## CHAPTER 5: DELICIOUS VEGAN DINNER RECIPES 97

| | |
|---|---|
| 1. SEXY VEGAN LENTIL STEW | 98 |
| 2. CHICKPEA FLOUR PANCAKES | 98 |
| 3. HIGH PROTEIN BLACK BEAN AND CORN SUMMER SALAD | 99 |
| 4. ARUGULA LENTIL SALAD | 99 |
| 5. VEGAN PEPPERONI PIZZA PANINI | 100 |
| 6. CRAZY QUICK WHITE BEAN SALAD | 100 |
| 7. THE QUINOA SALAD | 100 |
| 8. VEGETABLE ORZO SOUP | 101 |
| 9. VEGAN PEANUT NOODLES WITH CRISPY TOFU | 102 |
| 10. THE VEGGIE KING | 102 |
| 11. BEST VEGAN EGG SALAD SANDWICH | 103 |
| 12. CHICKPEA SUMMER SALAD | 103 |
| 13. AUTHENTIC MOROCCAN COUSCOUS SALAD | 104 |
| 14. HEARTS OF PALM CRAB-STYLE SALAD | 104 |
| 15. PEANUT NOODLE SALAD | 105 |
| 16. WHITE BEAN SALAD | 105 |
| 17. MEDITERRANEAN CHICKPEA SALAD | 106 |
| 18. RED PESTO PASTA | 106 |
| 19. BROCCOLI PESTO PASTA SALAD | 107 |
| 20. LOW CARB HIGH TASTE ZOODLES | 107 |
| 21. TURKISH LENTIL SALAD | 108 |
| 22. SMOKEY CHICKPEA LAVASH WRAP | 108 |
| 23. VEGAN BROCCOLI SALAD | 109 |
| 24. ASIAN TOFU SALAD | 110 |
| 25. CHICKPEA CURRY | 110 |
| 26. EASY CAPRESE SANDWICH | 111 |
| 27. SWEET & TANGY BUDDHA BOWL | 111 |
| 28. CHINESE SESAME TOFU WITH GARLIC GINGER SAUCE | 112 |
| 29. VEGAN EGG MAYO SANDWICH | 113 |
| 30. HEALTHY MASHED SWEET POTATO | 113 |
| 31. ASIAN STYLE CREAMY CORN SOUP | 114 |
| 32. ONE POT HUMMUS PASTA | 115 |
| 33. ASIAN SLAW VEGAN WRAPS WITH CAULIFLOWER RICE | 115 |
| 34. FABULOUS FALAFEL SALAD WITH FAKE TAHINI SAUCE | 116 |
| 35. VEGAN TUNA SALAD | 116 |
| 36. VEGETABLE BIRYANI | 117 |
| 37. WHOLE ROASTED CAULIFLOWER WITH TAHINI SAUCE | 117 |
| 38. FRANKIES | 118 |
| 39. SZECHUAN EGGPLANT | 119 |

| | |
|---|---|
| 40. VEGAN ALFREDO | 120 |
| 41. VEGAN BROCCOLI CHEDDAR JALAPENO SOUP | 121 |
| 42. BUTTERNUT SQUASH RISOTTO | 121 |
| 43. VEGAN TACOS WITH SMOKY CHIPOTLE PORTOBELLOS | 122 |
| 44. VEGAN SPAGHETTI AND BEETBALLS | 123 |
| 45. COCONUT MILLET BOWL WITH BERBERE SPICED SQUASH & CHICKPEAS | 124 |
| 46. VEGAN TIKKA MASALA | 125 |
| 47. CRISPY QUINOA CAKES WITH TOMATO CHICKPEA RELISH | 126 |
| 48. RAMEN WITH SHIITAKE BROTH | 127 |
| 49. FARMER'S MARKET FRIED RICE | 128 |
| 50. BAKED SHEET PAN RATATOUILLE | 128 |
| 51. OAXACAN BOWL | 129 |
| 52. ORECCHIETTE WITH CREAMY CARROT MISO SAUCE | 130 |
| 53. BLACK PEPPER TOFU WITH BOK CHOY | 131 |
| 54. INSTANT POT MUJADRA | 131 |
| 55. INSTANT POT LENTIL CURRY | 132 |
| 56. VEGGIE LO MEIN | 133 |
| 57. VEGAN TLAYUDAS | 134 |
| 58. SZECHUAN TOFU & VEGGIES | 135 |
| 59. MIDDLE EASTERN SALAD TACOS | 135 |
| 60. ROASTED PORTOBELLO STEAKS WITH WALNUT COFFEE SAUCE | 136 |
| 61. ZUCCHANOUSH | 136 |
| 62. CUCUMBER MELON SOUP | 137 |
| 63. TOFU PAD THAI | 137 |
| 64. SPICED FRESH TOMATO SOUP WITH SWEET & HERBY PITAS | 138 |
| 65. BBQ CHICKPEA & CAULIFLOWER FLATBREADS WITH AVOCADO MASH | 138 |
| 66. TAHINI LEMON QUINOA WITH ASPARAGUS RIBBONS | 139 |
| 67. ROASTED VEGGIES AND TEMPEH BOWL | 139 |
| 68. CRISPY POTATOES WITH VEGAN NACHO SAUCE | 140 |
| 69. ASIAN SESAME ZUCCHINI NOODLES | 140 |
| 70. CREAMY VEGAN LINGUINE WITH MILD MUSHROOMS | 141 |

**CONCLUSION** — **143**

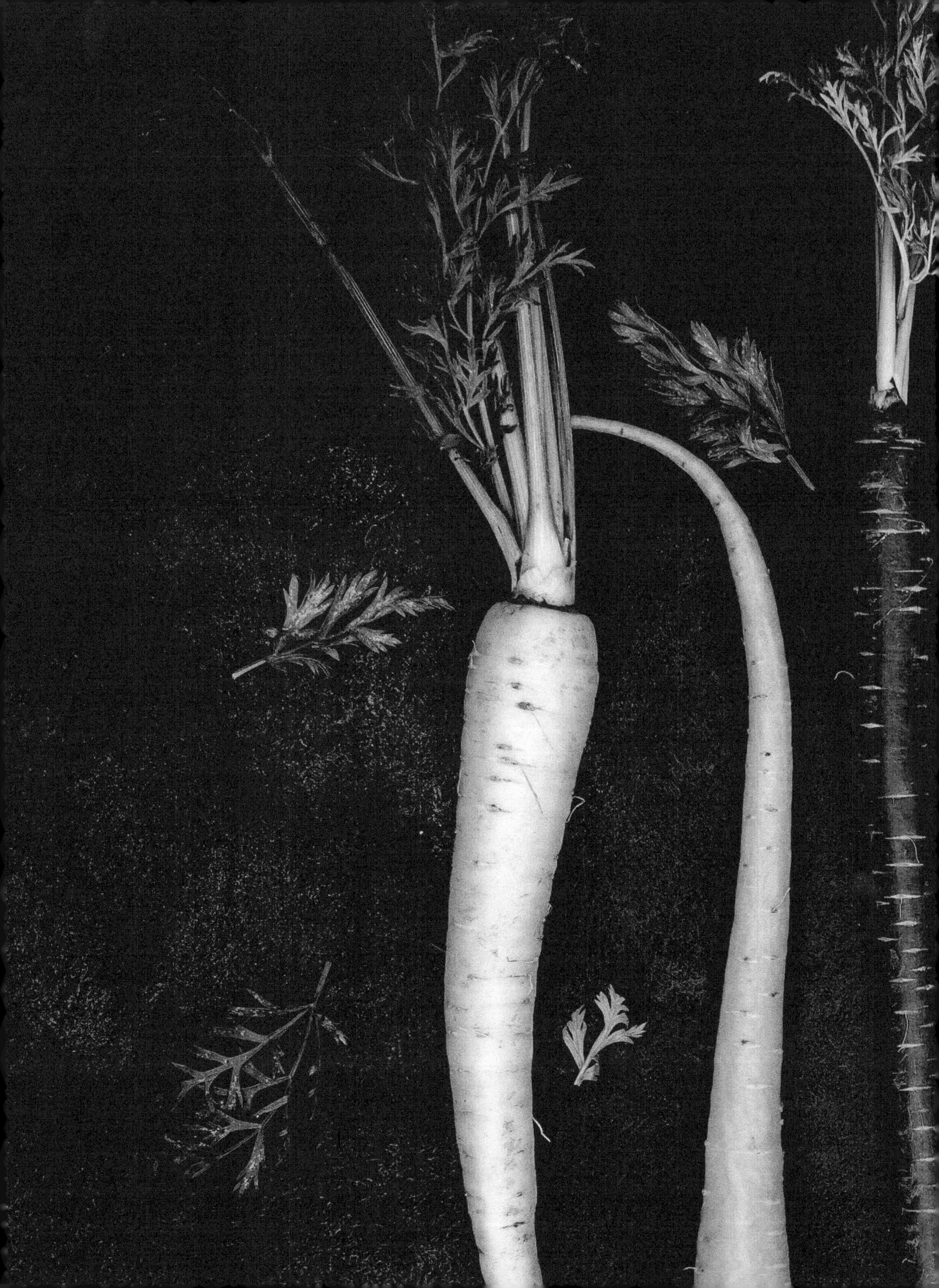

# INTRODUCTION

The Pegan Diet is a hybrid of two popular eating plans: the Paleo Diet as well as the Vegan Diet. The Paleo Diet is centered on our Paleolithic predecessors' eating patterns, and it exclusively contains items that would have been accessible prior to the invention of agriculture. The vegan diet aims to eliminate all kinds of animal exploitation & suffering, whether for food, clothing, or any other reason. As a result, the vegan diet excludes all animal protein, such as meat, eggs, & dairy. In reality, Pegan food combines the greatest nutritional elements of the vegan & Paleo diets, plus a bunch of other health advantages, including improved health, illness prevention, reduced inflammation, and increased vitality.

As a result, the two diets conflict with each other in many respects, although the Pegan diet's primary principle is an emphasis on genuine, whole foods. The goal is to limit processed foods by eating vegetables, fruits, hazelnuts, seeds, meats, fish, as well as eggs while avoiding dairy, cereals, lentils, sugar, & highly processed foods.

The Pegan diet forbids the consumption of conventionally raised meats & eggs. Rather than grass-fed, pasture-raised beef, bacon, chicken, and the whole eggs are prioritized. It also promotes the consumption of seafood, particularly those with minimal mercury levels, such as sardines & wild salmon.

Many nutrient-dense foods are restricted on the Pegan diet, partially because some individuals cannot handle them. While some individuals are lactose or gluten allergic or have difficulty digesting the fiber in beans, this isn't the case for the majority of people. If anybody continues the Pegan diet as they have difficulties with inflammation or digestion, it will also assist them in determining the underlying cause of their health issues.

Being on a diet does not really mean you have to eat healthily or limit yourself excessively; it just means you're changing your food patterns for the better. There are numerous diets available; however, many individuals find the process of choosing one to be daunting. The Pegan Diet is an excellent option if you want a diet with documented health advantages that is also simple to follow.

The Pegan Diet is a hybrid of two popular eating

plans: the Paleo Diet as well as the Vegan Diet. The Paleo Diet, as well as the Vegan Diet, are both founded on the idea of whole food nutrition, which entails eating only natural, unprocessed foods.

# CHAPTER 1: UNDERSTANDING THE PEGAN DIET

## 1.1 What Is Pegan Diet?

The "pegan" diet is a combination of the paleo diet (which emphasizes entire foods that may have been taken or obtained, such as fruits, vegetables, meats, and nuts) and the vegan diet (which concentrates only on plant-based meals).

The pegan diet incorporates important concepts from the paleo & vegan diets, with the goal of reducing inflammation, balancing blood sugar, and supporting optimum health. You're not the only one if you think being paleo and vegan at the same time seems almost impossible. The pegan diet, irrespective of the name, is different and follows its own list of rules. It's really less rigorous than a paleo / vegan diet on its own. The focus is on fruits and vegetables, although modest to moderate quantities of meat, some fish, almonds, seeds, as well as certain lentils are permitted. Sugars, oils, and cereals that have been overly processed are avoided, although they are still allowed in modest quantities.

The pegan diet isn't really intended to be followed for a short period of time. Instead, it tries to be more long-term, so you can stick with it forever.

## 1.2 Foods to Consume and Avoid

What to eat?

Natural foods, or types of food that have experienced with no or little preparation before accessing your plate, are emphasized in the pegan diet.

Plants should be consumed in large quantities.

Fruits and vegetables are the main food groups for the pegan diet, and they should contribute to 75 percent of your overall consumption. To reduce your blood sugar reaction, lower-glycemic fruits and veggies, including berries & non-starchy veggies, must be prioritized.

For individuals who have previously established appropriate blood sugar control without first doing the diet, small quantities of green veggies and sweet fruits may be permitted.

Stick to fats that have been lightly processed.

You should consume healthy fats from particular sources on this diet, like:

Nuts: Excluding peanuts

Seeds, with the exception of seed oils that have been processed

Olives and avocados: You can also use frozen olive as well as avocado oil.

Coconut: Coconut oil that has not been processed is allowed.

You may consume the following grains & legumes:

• Black rice, millet, amaranth, quinoa, and oats are examples of grains.

• Dried beans, chickpeas, black beans, and pinto beans are examples of legumes.

If you are diabetic or have another disease that causes poor blood sugar management, you should limit these items even more.

What not to eat?

As it allows for the occasional consumption of virtually any food, the pegan plan is far more adaptable than the paleo and vegan diets.

Certain foods and dietary categories, however, are severely discouraged. Based on who you ask, a few of these meals are considered to be toxic, although some are regarded as very nutritious.

On the pegan diet, these items are usually avoided:

Dairy products such as cow's milk, yogurt, as well

as cheese are highly avoided. Foods prepared from sheep and goat milk, on the other hand, are allowed in restricted amounts. Grass-fed butter is occasionally permitted.

Sugar: Sugar content in any form, processed or not, is generally avoided. It can be used sometimes, but only in moderation.

Oils: that have been refined or extensively processed, like canola, soybean, sunflower, as well as corn oil should nearly always be shunned.

Synthetic colorings, flavorings, preservatives, and other additions are not used in the food.

The majority of these items are off-limits owing to their potential to raise blood sugar and/or cause inflammation in the body.

## 1.3 Advantages and Disadvantages of Pegan Diet

Potential advantages

The pegan diet can help overall health in a variety of ways. Perhaps its greatest feature is its heavy focus on fruit & vegetable consumption.

Fruits and veggies provide a wide range of nutrients. They're high in fiber, vitamins, minerals, & plant compounds that have been known to decrease oxidative stress as well as inflammation and prevent illness.

Balanced, unsaturated fats from nuts, beans, and other plants are also emphasized in the pegan diet, which may benefit heart health. Additionally, diets that emphasize whole foods and exclude ultra-processed items are linked to better dietary quality.

Potential drawbacks

Despite its benefits, the pegan diet has certain disadvantages that should be considered.

Restrictions that aren't required

Whereas the pegan diet provides for more freedom than a vegan and paleo diet altogether, many of the suggested limitations exclude extremely nutritious items like legumes, healthy grains, as well as dairy excessively.

The elimination of these items is frequently cited by supporters of the pegan plan as a consequence of enhanced inflammation and higher blood sugar. Of course, some individuals have gluten as well as dairy sensitivities, which may cause inflammation. Likewise, while eating high-starch meals like grains and legumes, some individuals have trouble controlling their blood sugar.

Lessening certain foods may be acceptable in these situations. It is not essential to avoid them until you have particular allergies or aversions. Furthermore, if broad categories of foods are omitted haphazardly, nutritional shortages may result if those elements aren't properly supplied. As a result, a basic knowledge of nutrition may be required to properly follow the pegan diet.

Inaccessibility

While a diet rich in natural fruits, veggies, as well as grass-fed, pasture-raised animals may seem ideal in general, it may be out of reach for so many.

To be effective on a diet, you'll need a lot of time to prepare meals, some culinary and meal-planning expertise, plus access to a wide range of ingredients, some of which may be very costly. Dining out might also be challenging owing to limitations on popular packaged foods, like cooking oils. This may lead to feelings of social isolation or tension.

1.4 Why will you only find vegan recipes within this book?

This book is for those who want to approach the Pegan diet without animal products. As written previously, some animal products are allowed, but I chose not to include them to give all vegans the possibility to follow this diet without problems.

## 1.4 7 Day Meal Plan

The hardest thing about following a diet is scheduling meals. You never know what to eat, especially when you're just starting out because you're not yet familiar with the ingredients and dishes allowed. A perfect Meal Plan comes from dish choices for each meal of the day. This book is designed to facilitate the task of scheduling and allow you not to deviate and maintain your commitment to follow this diet without any effort.

The book has been constructed in a revolutionary way by dividing the recipes into Easy Breakfast Recipes, Vegan Drinks & Smoothies, Vegan Lunch Recipes, and Delicious Vegan Dinner Recipes so you can effortlessly choose what to eat at any time of the day.

In addition, I have selected simple recipes with few ingredients that are easy to find in any supermarket in your area.

Are you undecided about what to eat? No problem. Just take a random recipe for breakfast, one for lunch, one for dinner, and one for a possible snack, and enjoy. Just point your finger at the table of contents, open the correct page and prepare your dish. Following a diet has never been easier.

Below you can get an idea of what a typical week might look like. You don't have to follow it as written; just try the recipes inside the book and choose the ones you like best.

## DAY 1

Breakfast

- Dark Chocolate Quinoa Breakfast Bowl

Lunch

Minty Peas & Onions

- Chili-Lime Roasted Chickpeas
- Cabbage & Rutabaga Slaw

Dinner

- Salmon from the wild, topped with coconut flakes
- Asparagus sautéed
- Rainbow carrots sautéed

## DAY 2

Breakfast

- Steamed Wild Rice with Toasted Hazelnut Butter
- Avocado

Lunch

- Homemade Potato Chips
- Crunchy Breadsticks
- Warm tasty Greens with Garlic

Dinner

- Cucumber Melon Soup
- Tofu Pad Thai

## DAY 3

Breakfast

- Vegan Gingerbread Scones with Vanilla Bean Glaze
- Pecan Pie Overnight Oats

Lunch

- Vegan Tomato Tart
- Stuffed Roast pumpkin

Dinner

- Ramen with Shiitake Broth
- Farmer's Market Fried Rice

## DAY 4

Breakfast

- Easy Canned Peaches
- Flaxseed Blueberry Oatmeal

Lunch

- Pasta Nourish Bowl
- Sweet Potato Noodles with Crispy Kale

Dinner

- Vegan Alfredo
- Vegan Broccoli Cheddar Jalapeno Soup
- Butternut Squash Risotto

## DAY 5

Breakfast

- Vegan Pumpkin Bread
- Old-Fashioned Oatmeal

Lunch
- Spicy Grilled Eggplant
- Simple Guacamole

Dinner
- Crispy Potatoes with Vegan Nacho Sauce
- Asian Sesame Zucchini Noodles
- Creamy Vegan Linguine with Mild Mushrooms

- Crazy Quick White bean Salad

## DAY 6

Breakfast
- Beet & Blood Orange Spice Smoothie
- Avocado Toast

Lunch
- Arrabbiata Beans
- Roasted Cauliflower Garlic Hummus
- Best Dry Sautéed Mushrooms

Dinner
- Vegan Spaghetti and Beetballs
- Coconut Millet Bowl with Berbere Spiced Squash & Chickpeas
- Brussels sprouts

## DAY 7

Breakfast
- Golden Peach Sunrise Smoothie
- Pistachio & Cardamom Butter

Lunch
- Arroz Verde - Mexican Green Rice
- Non-Creamy Potato Salad

Dinner
- Vegan Pepperoni Pizza Panini

# PEGAN DIET PLAN EXAMPLE

## EVERY DAY EAT:

**5 + cups vegetables:**
Choose any-suggested:
- Non-starchy veggies: Asparagus, Broccoli, Kale

**4 carbs:**
Choose either fruit, grains or starchy veggies:
- Starchy veggies: Sweet potatoes, Squash, Corn
- (1/2 cup grains, 1 piece Bread, ½ cup Oats)

**3 proteins:**
3 servings of protein:
- 3 vegan proteins: 1 cup Beans, Tofu, Tempeh, Seeds

**2 fats:**
Choose from:
¼ Avocado, 1 tbsp Oil, 1 oz. Nuts, 1 tbsp Nut butter

**1 dairy substitute:**
Choose from:
Nut milk, Non-dairy yogurt, Nut cheese

## WHAT DOES IT LOOK LIKE:

**Breakfast**
Avocado Toast:
- 1 slice of whole grain toast
- ¼ Avocado

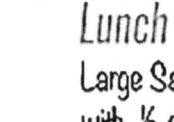

**Lunch**
Large Salad with ½ cup Beans

**Dinner**
1 cup Cauliflower rice, 3 oz Protein

**Snack**
Handful of strawberries

**Snack**
1 Cucumber
1 oz. Nuts

## RULES:

**Alcohol**
2 drinks per week
(1 drink = 1 glass of wine, 1 cup of beer, oz. of liquor)

**Dessert**
Twice per week

**EXERCISE**
30 minutes a day, 3 days a week

### PLUS! ONE CHEAT DAY PER WEEK

## CHAPTER 2:
## EASY BREAKFAST RECIPES

# 1. CRISPY HASH BROWN HAYSTACKS

Serving: 12

Preparation time: 50 min

Nutritionalvalues:Calories-60kcal|Carbs-10g|Protein-1g|Fat-2g

## Ingredients

- 4 cups shredded russet potatoes, gently packed
- 1 medium shallot, cut extremely thinly
- 1/2 cup of fresh or bottled corn (drained thoroughly if canned/do not freeze)
- 2 tablespoons vegan butter
- 1 tablespoon arrowroot starch/cornstarch (for binding)

## Directions

- Preheat the oven at 375 degrees F (190 degrees C) and place a rack in the midst. Also, prepare a regular muffin pan with oil of preference and line it with paper liners (to avoid sticking) (for flavor).

- Toss shredded potatoes, shallot, parsley, canned corn, heated vegan butter, cornstarch, salt, & pepper together in a wide mixing bowl.

- Fill each pan with approximately 1/4 cup of a mixture of potato and divide equally between twelve muffin tins. To form, softly press down. Bake for 20 min after adding a sprinkle of salt & pepper to the tops.

- Raise the oven temperature about 425 ⁰ (218 degrees C) at the 20-minute point and bake for another 10 to 12 minutes, or unless the tops are lightly browned, and the sides are deep golden brown.

- Remove from the oven and let aside for 5 minutes before using a butter knife to release the edges and carefully pull out with a spatula. Serve immediately, either plain or with a sprinkling of hot sauce.

- When it's fresh, it's the best. To freeze, place cooked haystacks on a baking tray in a thin layer and place in the freezer until solid. Then freeze for 3-4 weeks in an airtight container. Reheat in the oven until well warmed.

# 2. DARK CHOCOLATE QUINOA BREAKFAST BOWL

Serving: 4

Preparation time: 30 min

Nutritionalvalues:Calories-236kcal|Carbs-41g|Protein-7g|Fat-6g

## Ingredients

- 1 cup of white quinoa, uncooked
- 1 cup of almond milk (unsweetened)
- 2 tbsp. chocolate powder, unsweetened
- 2–3 tablespoons maple or coconut sugar
- Vegan dark chocolate, 3 to 4 squares (coarsely chopped)

## Directions

- Wash quinoa well in a thin mesh sieve for two min, then sift through and take out any remaining discolored bits or stones with your fingertips.

- Over moderate flame, heat a medium saucepan. When the pan is heated, add the rinsed and strained quinoa, then toast for three minutes, often turning to dry out any excess water and toast considerably.

- Pour almond & coconut milk, as well as a sprinkle of salt, and whisk. Bring to a simmer over high temperature, then lower to a medium simmer & cook for 20 to 25 min, open, stirring regularly. Increase the temperature to medium-low if it no longer simmers. Throughout the cooking process, keep the temperature at a low simmer.

- Take out from heat after the liquid has been evaporated & the quinoa is soft, then stir in the chocolate powder, maple syrup, also vanilla. To mix, stir everything together.

• Taste the meal and make any necessary adjustments to the taste. Add a little extra milk (almond) if you like the consistency thinner.

• Garnish with a tiny piece of vegan chocolate or any other preferred toppings in each dish of quinoa.

## 3. BUCKWHEAT CREPES

Serving: 12

Preparation time: 25 min

Nutritional values: Calories-71kcal|Carbs-8g|Protein-1g|Fat-3g

### Ingredients

• 1 cup of buckwheat flour, untoasted (raw)
• Flaxseed meal, 3/4 tablespoon
• 1 3/4 cup of light (canned) milk made from coconut
• 1/8 teaspoon cinnamon powder (optional; eliminate for savory)
• Sweetener (to taste)

### Directions

• Combine buckwheat flour, flaxseed meal, light (packaged) coconut milk, salt as per taste, oil (avocado), cinnamon (ignore for savory), plus sweetener of preference to a blender or medium bowl (omit for savory or unsweetened).

• To combine, whirl in a blender or stir in a mixing bowl. The mixture should be capable of being poured but not runny. If the mixture is too thin, add a little more buckwheat flour. Thin with additional dairy-free milk if it's too dense.

• Over moderate flame, warm a cast-iron/non-stick skillet. (While a non-stick pan is recommended for crepes. When the pan is heated, drizzle in less oil and distribute into an equal layer. Allow the oil to heat until it is very hot; a drop of water would crackle as well as evaporate nearly instantly when thrown into the pan.

• 1/4 cup of batter should be added. Allow simmering until the top is bubbling as well as the edges have dried out (similar to pancakes). Cook for another 2-3 min on each side after gently flipping. If the food is cooking too fast, reduce the heat.

• Continue once all crepes are ready. After the first crepe, we didn't need to add any additional oil. Heat among parchment paper layers or on a platter under a cloth.

• Serve alone or with vegan or nut butter, syrup of maple, compote, or your favorite fillings.

## 4. PEANUTBUTTER & JELLY CHIA PUDDING

Serving: 3

Preparation time: 1 hr. 30 min

Nutritional values: Calories-211kcal|Carbs-19g|Protein-6g|Fat-13g

### Ingredients

For compote

• 1 cup of blueberries (wild) (frozen or fresh)
• 1 tablespoon of orange juice & chia seeds

For pudding

• 1 cup of almond milk, sugar-free
• 1/2 cup of coconut milk (mild)
• 1 to 2 tablespoons maple syrup (as per taste)
• 3 tablespoons salted natural peanut butter (creamy and fudgy / + extra for serving)

### Directions

• Bring the blueberries & orange juice to a medium skillet or saucepan. Heat over moderate flame until it begins to bubble. Reduce to medium-low heat and simmer for 2 minutes, stirring periodically. Remove the pan from the heat and stir in the chia seeds. To mix, stir everything together.

- Distribute the compote into three small serving plates and refrigerate until ready to serve.

- Meanwhile, combine almond & coconut milk, vanilla (preferred), maple syrup, as well as peanut butter in a processor. To thoroughly mix, blend on medium. Taste and modify the tastes as required, pouring more maple syrup as well as peanut butter for sweet taste and saltiness, respectively.

- Process a few times to integrate the chia seeds, becoming careful not to mix them since you want the seeds to remain intact.

- Place in a fluid measuring cup/jar in the refrigerator to start chilling (or simply put the entire blender in the fridge).

- Allow the compote (chia) to settle for ten min. Then, take the chia pudding & compote out of the fridge. Mix the chia pudding to disperse the seeds, and divide among the 3 serving plates directly on the upper edge of the compote.

- Cover tightly and refrigerate for at least 1 to 2 hours (ideally overnight), or until completely cold and pudding-like in texture.

- Top with additional peanut butter as well as fresh blueberries to serve (optional). Will keep in the freezer for 3 to 4 days if covered.

## 5. RAW-NOLA

Serving: 14

Preparation time: 5 min

Nutritional values: Calories-139kcal|Carbs-11g|Protein-4g|Fat-10g

### Ingredients

- 1 1/2 cup of walnuts, uncooked

- 1 heaping Tablespoon hemp seeds 15–17 flattened dates (Medjool)

- 1 tablespoon flaxseed meal & chia seeds

- 1/2 cup of unsweetened grated coconut

- 1/2 cup of rolled oats (gluten-free)

### Directions

- Put nuts in a food blender and pulse for a few minutes to coarsely chop them. Now add the dates & whirl 5 times to mix loosely.

- Pulse in the rest of the ingredients to mix. The finished product should reflect chunky granola.

- You may now add more "flavor" in the form of cacao powder plus nibs, dry fruit of your preference, or vanilla essence or powder.

- Serve plain, with coconut milk over, or with dairy-free cream! This granola might work in almost any situation where normal granola would.

- Keep leftovers at ambient temperature for two weeks or even in the fridge for up to three days in a sealed jar. Place in the freezer to keep for a longer period of time (up to one month).

## 6. ROASTED SWEET POTATO & KALE BREAKFAST HASH

Serving: 2

Preparation time: 45 min

Nutritional values: Calories-139kcal|Carbs-11g|Protein-4g|Fat-10g

### Ingredients

- 8 oz. tofu (extra-firm)

- 2 tiny sweet potatoes (or 1 big sweet potato / two medium sweet potatoes/cut into large pieces, skin on / natural if possible)

- 3 1/4 teaspoon tandoori masala (divided)

- 1 onion, red (skin & tips removed, then cut crosswise into wedges)

- 1 large kale bunch (diced, large stems discarded)

## Directions

- Preheat oven to 400 degrees F (204 degrees C). To squeeze out excess liquid, cover tofu in a tidy towel and place anything weighty on top (including a cast-iron pan).

- Meanwhile, sprinkle sweet potatoes with half tablespoon oil, 1 teaspoon tandoori masala seasoning, 1 teaspoon coconut sugar, and a sprinkle of salt & pepper. Toss to evenly coat.

- Sprinkle onion with 1/2 tablespoon oil, 1/4 teaspoon tandoori seasoning, and a sprinkle of salt & pepper  Toss to evenly coat.

- Bake the onions as well as potatoes for 25 to 35 minutes total, turning halfway through to ensure uniform cooking. Once the onions are golden and roasted, as well as the sweet potatoes are spoon soft, they're done. Remove the dish from the oven and put it aside.

- While the veggies are roasting, smash the pressed tofu with two forks in a mixing bowl. Sprinkle with chopped parsley, turmeric, as well as a hefty sprinkle of salt and pepper to taste. Place aside.

- Heat a wide pan over medium-high heat after the potatoes as well as onions are nearly done cooking. Add half tbsp. oil, tofu, & 1 teaspoon tandoori masala seasoning. To dry & color the tofu, cook for five min, stirring periodically. Then take it out of the skillet and put it aside.

- Add the rest 1/2 tablespoon oil to the pan and the kale  Mix with a sprinkle of salt and pepper, as well as 1 teaspoon tandoori masala spice mix, and stir to coat. Fry the kale for 3-4 min, often turning to sear and wilt it.

- Push the greens to one corner of the skillet and reheat the tofu.  Turn off the heat but leave the pan on the stove.

- To serve, split the kale between two (or three) serving dishes, then top with the roasted sweet potatoes as well as onion, followed by the tofu. Enjoy the rest of the chopped parsley. Serve with a large scoop of hummus and a dash of hot sauce for added flavor (optional).

# 7. SAVORY BREAKFAST SALAD

Serving: 2

Preparation time: 20 min

Nutritional values: Calories-523kcal|Carbs-58g|Protein-7g|Fat-38g

## Ingredients

- 2 small sweet potatoes (can substitute 1 big sweet potato for Two smalls / sliced into 1/4-inch patties then half / organic if available)

- 4 cups of endive and/or assorted greens

- Lemon juice, 3 tablespoons

- 1 cup of blueberries

- 4 tablespoons hummus (60 g) split

## Directions

- Over moderate flame, heat a wide skillet. Stir in the oil (and water), sweet potatoes (diced), salt, & pepper once the pan is heated. To guarantee uniform cooking, stack in a thin layer and cover with a lid to steam.

- Cook for a total of 3-4 minutes. The potatoes should then be covered and turned to ensure equal cooking. Reduce heat to medium-low if browning is occurring too fast. Cook for another 10-15 minutes, or until light brown on each side and soft.

- Meanwhile, make the vinaigrette by tossing or whisking together the juice of lemon, olive oil, salt, as well as pepper in a tiny jar or mixing plate. Taste and adjust the seasonings as required, using more lemon for sharpness, oil for richness, or salt and black pepper for overall taste. Place aside.

- To serve, split the greens among serving dishes and garnish with toasted sweet potatoes, berries (blue), avocados, hummus, hemp seeds (if desired), as well as chopped parsley (optional). The dressing should be served on the side.

- Eat right away. Portions will keep for 2 to 3 days if kept separate from the dressing but are best when served immediately.

## 8. CHOCOLATE CHIP OATMEAL COOKIE PANCAKE

Serving: 2

Preparation time: 23 min

Nutritional values: Calories-472kcal|Carbs-60g|Protein-9g|Fat-23g

### Ingredients

- 1 flax egg mixture & 1 medium banana, extremely ripe
- A half teaspoon of vanilla extract
- 1 tablespoon of almond butter
- 1/3 cup of almond milk, unsweetened
- 2 tablespoons almond flour (made from organic almonds)

### Directions

- In a wide mixing bowl, combine flaxseed meal as well as water and let aside for 3 to 5 minutes.
- Mix the extremely ripe banana with baking powder.
- Stir in the oil, salt, extract of vanilla, almond butter, as well as almond milk.
- Whisk oats, almond meal, as well as gluten-free flour mix in a mixing bowl until just incorporated.
- After that, carefully mix in the chocolate chunks. Allow for 5 minutes of resting time while preheating the skillet to medium-low heat. It should be heated, but not too warm. Otherwise, the pancakes will be burned - approximately 300-325 degrees.
- Drop 1/4 cup of batter onto a lightly oiled skillet and spread slightly to form a pancake design. Sauté for 3 to 4 min each side, or until lightly brown on both sides. When bubbles develop on top as well as the edges look dry, they're ready to break.
- Serve with a sprinkle of maple syrup, then a few more chocolate chips, if desired. Leftovers reheat nicely in the microwave.

## 9. DARK CHOCOLATE GRANOLA

Serving: 9

Preparation time: 34 min

Nutritional values: Calories-364kcal|Carbs-45g|Protein-8g|Fat-19g

### Ingredients

- 3 cups of rolled oats (gluten-free)
- 1 cup of raw nuts, crushed (ideally cashews, almonds, and/or hazelnuts)
- 1/4 cup crushed or dried coconut (unsweetened)
- 3 tablespoons pure cane sugar plus coconut sugar
- Cocoa powder, 1/3 cup
- 1/2 cup of dark chocolate pieces or chips (vegan)

### Directions

- Preheat the oven at 340 degrees Fahrenheit (171 C).
- Combine the oats, almonds, coconut, chia seeds, sugar (coconut), salt, & cocoa powder in a blender (or mixing dish). To mix, press a few seconds (or stir).
- Heat the coconut oil as well as maple syrup in a pan over medium heat until warmed and mixed. Pour the liquid over the dried ingredients, then whisk thoroughly. If you use a food proces-

sor, the oats and nuts will be broken down a little more, resulting in a smoother consistency, but this is an alternative.

- Put the mixture uniformly on a baking tray (or several baking sheets if preparing a large quantity), then bake for 17 to 24 min (or until aromatic & nicely browned), stirring halfway through to ensure equal baking.

- Allow cooling fully before serving. After that, pour the chocolate (optional). It should preserve for several weeks if placed in an airtight container with an airtight seal. Alternatively, freeze for up to a month or longer.

## 10. ROASTED RAINBOW VEGETABLE BOWL

Serving: 2

Preparation time: 30 min

Nutritional values: Calories-519kcal|Carbs-59g|Protein-13g|Fat-28g

### Ingredients

- 3-4 large red / yellow baby potatoes (1/4 pieces)
- 2 carrots, medium (halved & thinly sliced)
- 1 medium beet, thinly sliced (1/8-inch pieces)
- 4 medium-sized radishes (halved)
- 1 cup of broccoli and cabbage (coarsely chopped)
- 2 cups of collard greens/kale, diced (organic when possible)
- 2 tablespoons tahini & hemp seeds (divided)

### Directions

- Preheat the oven at 400 degrees Fahrenheit (204 degrees Celsius), and prepare two baking trays with parchment paper.
- Sprinkle 1/2 of the oil (or water), powder (curry), as well as sea salt over the baby potatoes, sweet potatoes, diced carrots, beets, as well as radishes on one baking tray. Toss everything together. Cook for 20 to 25 minutes, or until lightly browned and soft.

- Put the cabbage, diced bell pepper, & broccoli on the other baking tray. Pour the rest half of the oil (or water), powder of curry, as well, as sea salt over the top. Toss everything together.

- Put the other pan in the oven after the potatoes/carrots have reached the ten-minute mark and cook for a maximum of 15 to 20 minutes. Toss the collard greens/kale into each pan in the final five min of baking and cook until soft and vibrant green.

- To start serving, distribute the veggies among serving plates and top with avocado (if desired), juice of lemon, tahini and hemp seeds, and a sprinkle of sea salt... You may also top with other fresh herbs

- When it's fresh, it's the best. Refrigerate leftovers for 3 to 4 days if covered.

## 11. BANANA WALNUT PANCAKES

Serving: 14

Preparation time: 30 min

Nutritional values: Calories-240kcal|Carbs-35g|Protein-6g|Fat-9g

### Ingredients

- 2 cups of oat flour (gluten-free)
- Almond flour (1/2 cup)
- 2 bananas, slightly ripe
- 1 1/2 tablespoons extract of vanilla
- 2 1/2 tablespoons of maple syrup
- Non-dairy milk, 2 1/4 cup
- 3/4 cup of raw walnuts, diced

## Directions

- Mix oat flour, flour (gluten-free), almond flour, powder of baking, salt, cinnamon, ginger (preferred), as well as nutmeg to a large mixing bowl (optional).

Set aside after whisking everything together.

- Add the bananas to a different mixing container and mash them. Then mix together the heated coconut oil, extract of vanilla, maple syrup, as well as non-dairy milk. It's not a major problem if the coconut oil solidifies or clumps. To remelt, heat for 45 seconds to 1 minute in the microwave; otherwise, continue.

- Combine the wet & dry ingredients in a large mixing bowl and gently mix everything together. Then fold/mix in the crushed walnuts & oats unless the batter is thoroughly mixed. It should have a thick consistency yet be smooth and creamy.

- Over moderate flame, heat a wide non-stick skillet, pan, or cast-iron griddle. Carefully spread coconut oil / vegan butter into the skillet.

- When the skillet is heated, pour 1/3 to 1/4 cup of the mixture into it. Cook for 2 minutes, or until bubbles form on the top of the pancakes and the sides look dry. Turn the pancakes gently and cook for another 2 minutes, or unless browned on the bottom.

- Prepared pancakes should be transferred to a baking tray or plate & kept warm in a 200°F (94°C) oven. Bake until all of the batter is being used up, approximately 14 to 16 pancakes.

- These pancakes are great on their own, but with vegan butter and peanut butter, diced bananas, granola, flakes of coconut, and maple syrup, they're even better. To avoid sticking, keep chilled leftover crepes (without sprinkles) in a container divided with wax/parchment paper. Retains for four days in the fridge and 1 month in the freezer. Reheat until warm in a toaster oven or in the oven

.

# 12. SPICY TEMPEH BREAKFAST SAUSAGE

Serving: 5

Preparation time: 2 hr. 30 min

Nutritional values: Calories-156kcal|Carbs-7g|Protein-8g|Fat-11g

## Ingredients

- Tempeh, 8 oz.
- 1/4 white onion (medium) (chopped)
- 4 garlic cloves (finely chopped / 4 cloves = 2 tablespoons)
- 1/4 teaspoon of red pepper flakes (extra for spicy sausage)
- 2 tablespoons Worcestershire sauce (vegan)

## Directions

- Finely diced the tempeh and combined it with the other ingredients in a mixing

container (or a blender).

- Mix well with tidy hands (or whiz in a blender) until completely mixed. The consistency should be similar to that of sausage.

- Taste a tiny quantity and adjust the seasoning as required, using more cayenne pepper as well as red pepper flakes for spice, salt and black pepper for whole taste, brown sugar for sweetener, or paprika for smoky flavor if desired.

- To enable the flavors to emerge, wrap & refrigerate for a minimum of 2 hours, ideally 24 hours, or up to three days.

- Cover a 1/3 cup of measuring cup with "sausage" and cover with aluminum foil or parchment paper while ready to cook. Cover with plastic wrap/parchment paper and press down. Then carefully take it from the pan and place it on a clean platter. Make a 1/2-inch wide disc by pressing down. Continue unless the batter is finished - approximately five "sausages."

• Over moderate flame, heat a large skillet. Once the pan is heated, add 1-2 Tablespoons oil (or sufficient to cover the surface) and just as many fillets as the pan will easily hold. Season with a pinch of salt and pepper.

• Cook for 3 to 4 minutes, or until golden on the underside. Then carefully turn (they're delicate) and cook for another 3 to 4 minutes, or unless the bottom is browned.

• Serve right away. Refrigerate leftovers for up to 3 days or freeze them for up to one month. You may also prepare the patties beforehand (up to one month), store them uncooked, & then cook them.

## 13. CRISPY EGGPLANT BACON

Serving: 14

Preparation time: 40 min

Nutritional values: Calories-21kcal|Carbs-3g|Protein-0.4g|Fat-1g

### Ingredients

• 1 medium eggplant, cut in half (you'll only need half of it)

• 1 1/2 tablespoons of tamari

• 1 tablespoon vegan Worcestershire sauce & 1 tablespoon maple syrup

• 2 tablespoons liquid smoke

• 1 teaspoon garlic powder

### Directions

• Heat up the oven at 250 degrees F. Prepare one large or two medium baking trays with parchment paper.

• Cut eggplant in halves horizontally and put aside one piece for later. Then, to make two long, thin pieces, chop the rest of the eggplant in half horizontally once more.

• Using a mandolin, cut into extremely thin strips that resemble bacon in size & shape. They might be somewhat thicker than sheet thin, with a thickness of less than one-eighth inch. If the pieces are too wide, they may struggle to tenderize and/or take relatively more time. Place aside.

• In a large mixing bowl, whisk together the oil (avocado), tamari, Worcestershire sauce, syrup (maple), smoke (liquid), paprika, sea salt, powder of garlic, & black pepper.

• Coat all ends of the eggplant pieces with a sauce using a brush (or a spatula). Sprinkle with additional black pepper and place in a thin layer on the prepared baking sheet(s).

• Bake for 25 to 30 minutes, then turn the eggplant pieces and bake for another 5 to15 minutes (or more if the pieces are thicker), or unless the eggplant is dark red, dried, and somewhat crispy. Lower temperature and cook longer to dehydration if browning is excessive but not crunchy. Take out from the oven & set aside to cool for a few minutes. The further it cools, the crispier it will get.

• Use right away on sandwiches, salads, or as an accompaniment to or incorporated into a vegan scramble.

## 14. CANDIED ORANGE PEEL GRANOLA

Serving: 4

Preparation time: 1 hr. 30 min

Nutritional values: Calories-239kcal|Carbs-29g|Protein-5g-|Fat-11g

### Ingredients

• Oranges weighing 3 lbs.

• 1 (12-oz.) package granola

• 3 cups of sugar

• 3 oz. diced dark chocolate

• Yogurt, plain

• Segments of clementine

## Directions

- Cut scrape from 3 pounds. (4 - 5) navel oranges; chop into 1/4-inch strands. Simmer in water for one min. Reduce heat to low and cook for 10 minutes. Drain and repeat the process two more times.

- Boil 2 cups sugar as well as 2 cups water until the sugar is dissolved. Cook, bring to a simmer until the peel begins to turn translucent, approximately 1 hour; drain.

- Allow 4 hours for the peel to dry but remain sticky on a wire rack. Mix with one cup sugar and set aside on a cooling rack for 1 day or until fully dry.

- Bring 3/4 cup diced peel to 1 (12-ounce) pack almond granola as well as 3 oz. diced dark chocolate.

- End up serving with clementine slices as well as plain yogurt.

## 15. CRUNCHY ALMOND GRANOLA

Serving: 12

Preparation time: 1 hr.

Nutritional values: Calories-230kcal|Carbs-28g|Protein-4g-|Fat-12g

### Ingredients

- 1/2 cup light brown sugar, sealed
- 1 tsp. of vanilla extract (pure)
- 4 cups of oats (old-fashioned)
- 1 cup of almonds
- 1/2 cup pepitas/sunflower seeds

### Directions

- Preheat the oven to 350 degrees Fahrenheit. The non-stick foil should be used to line two circular baking sheets.

- Stir together the brown sugar, extract of vanilla, oil and salt in a large mixing bowl. Toss in the oats, almonds, as well as sunflower seeds, ensuring sure they are thoroughly covered. Distribute the mixture between the two pans that have been prepared.

- Cook for 20 to 25 minutes, turning once, till lightly browned and crisp. Allow cooling fully before serving.

- The granola may be kept at ambient temperature for up to two weeks.

- Fill large mason jars with the prepared granola.

## 16. FARRO-AND-TOMATO SALAD WITH CRISPY CAPERS

Serving: 8

Preparation time: 20 min

Nutritional values: Calories-60kcal|Carbs-0g|Protein-0g|Fat-7g

### Ingredients

- Farro, 1 1/2 cup
- 3 tablespoons capers, patted dry
- 2 cups of flat-leaf parsley, fresh
- sherry vinegar, 3 tablespoons
- 1 1/2-pound grape & cherry tomatoes, peeled and halved

### Directions

- Cook farro as directed on the packet.

- In a large skillet, heat one tablespoon of oil over moderate flame. Cook for 1 to 2 minutes, unless capers are crisp. Place on a platter lined with paper towels. Cook parsley in 2 batches in the same pan until crisp; move to dish with capers, pouring more oil to saucepan between batches if required.

- In a mixing dish, combine the vinegar as well as the rest 2 tbsp. oil. Using salt and pepper, season to taste.

- Toss in the tomatoes & farro to mix. Just before dishing out, sprinkle with crunchy capers and parsley.

## 17. PEANUTBUTTER BANANA BREAD GRANOLA

Serving: 6

Preparation time: 50 min

Nutritional values: Calories-131kcal|Carbs-17g|Protein-4g|Fat-6g

### Ingredients

- 3 cups of rolled oats (old-fashioned)
- 1 cup lightly crumbled banana chips
- 1/2 cup Quinoa, uncooked
- 1/3 cup organic creamy peanut butter
- 1/4 cup pure honey

### Directions

- Preheat the oven to 325 degrees Fahrenheit. Using parchment paper, prepare 2 large rimmed baking pans. In a mixing bowl, combine the oats, crumbled banana chips, peanuts, uncooked quinoa, sugar, cinnamon, as well as salt.

- In a small pan, melt the butter & peanut butter with the honey over a moderate flame, often stirring, for 2 to 4 minutes. Remove the pan from the heat and mix in the banana & vanilla extract. Stir in the oat mixture until everything is well mixed.

- Distribute granola onto baking pans that have been lined with parchment paper. Bake for 25 to 27 minutes, turning pans periodically until lightly browned.

- Chill on wire racks after removing from pans. Break up the granola and store it in an airtight jar for up to a week.

## 18. GRAB AND GO CRANBERRY GRANOLA BARS

Serving: 16

Preparation time: 30 min

Nutritional values: Calories-200kcal|Carbs-30g|Protein-4g|Fat-9g

### Ingredients

- 1/2 cup honey
- 2 cups old-fashioned oats
- 2 egg whites, medium
- wheat germ (about 3/4 cup)
- 3/4 cup walnuts, chopped

### Directions

- Preheat the oven to 325°F. Using non-stick cooking spray, coat a 13-by-9-inch metal baking dish. Spray foil and line pan with it, providing a 2-inch overhang. Distribute 2 cups of old-fashioned oats on a dish; microwave on highest in one-minute intervals for 4 - 5 minutes, or until aromatic and brown, stirring periodically. Allow cooling. Stir honey, oil (vegetable), water, whites of eggs, lighter-colored sugar, ground cinnamon, as well as 1/2 tsp. salt together in a large mixing bowl until thoroughly combined. Return to the heated pan after folding in oats & roasted wheat germ, diced walnuts, then dried cranberries. Spread into an even layer with moist hands.

- Preheat oven to 350°F and bake for 28–30 minutes, or until lightly browned. Cool on a wire rack in the pan. Move to cut the board with foil and slice it into sixteen bars. Refrigerate for up to four days or freeze for up to one month in an airtight container.

## 19. STEAMED WILD RICE WITH TOASTED HAZELNUT BUTTER

Serving: 8

Preparation time: 55 min

Nutritional values: Calories-372kcal|Carbs-83g|Protein-7g|Fat-12g

### Ingredients

- 1 cup of hazelnuts
- 2 cups of wild rice
- 4 garlic cloves
- 4 fresh thyme sprigs
- 8 tablespoons butter

### Directions

- Preheat the oven to 350 degrees Fahrenheit. Arrange hazelnuts in an equal layer on a baking tray. Toast for 12 - 15 minutes, or until nicely browned. To remove the skins, cover the nuts in a fresh tea towel and massage them together. Remove the skins from the nuts and place them in a Ziploc bag to crush roughly with a pin. Set aside the nuts.

- Wash the wild rice. Mix rice, four cups water, cloves of garlic, dried bay leaves & thyme, as well as salt to a simmer in a wide, heavy saucepan over medium-high heat. Cook for 20 to 25 minutes, covered, over low heat, until water has evaporated and grains are soft and curved into a "C" form.

- Meanwhile, melt butter in a small pan over moderate heat, constantly stirring, for 3 to 5 minutes, or until it becomes golden brown. Stir in the parsley and nuts that have been set aside. Serve immediately with the reserved rice and hazelnut butter.

## 20. MAPLE-CITRUS SALAD WITH COCONUT

Serving: 8

Preparation time: 15 min

Nutritional values: Calories-90kcal|Carbs-7g|Protein-0g|Fat-5g

### Ingredients

- 2 grapefruits, large pink
- 2 navel oranges, medium
- 2 oranges (blood)
- 6 tbsp. freshly shredded coconut
- 2 tablespoons tarragon (fresh)

### Directions

- Over a mixing bowl, place a fine-mesh strainer. To remove segments from grapefruits as well as one navel orange, cut between membranes & place in strainer; move segments to a wide plate. Squeeze any leftover juice from the membranes of the citrus fruits into a strainer. Set aside the juice bowl. Cut the rest navel orange, oranges (blood), as well as lime into 1/4-inch wide rounds and arrange them on top of the grapefruit & orange segments on the plate.

- Mix 1/2 cup saved juice and maple syrup in a mixing bowl. Over the citrus, pour the syrup concoction. (Citrus may be kept in the fridge for up to one day if covered.) Toss the citrus with a light coating of coconut. Before serving, sprinkle with tarragon.

## 21. QUICK TANGELO MARMALADE

Serving: 3

Preparation time: 1 hr. 30 min

Nutritional values: Calories-66kcal|Carbs-12g|Protein-0g|Fat-0g

## Ingredients

- 3 lbs. tangelos
- 4 cups of sugar
- One vanilla bean
- 1 cup of water
- 1/2 apple, Granny Smith

## Directions

- Tangos should be washed and quartered. Use a handheld juicer to juice the fruit over a mixing bowl.
- Remove the peels from the juiced pieces and discard them. Discard the remainder of the fruit after slicing the peels into 1/4-inch-wide ribbons. Crack vanilla bean as well as put seeds into a small dish.
- Mix the juice, rinds, vanilla pod & seeds, sugar, water, as well as Granny Smith apple in a medium Dutch oven. Bring to a simmer, then drop to low heat & continue to cook, stirring periodically, for approximately 1 hour, or until the rinds are soft and the liquid has thickened. Remove the apple and vanilla bean pods and toss them out.
- Allow 1 hour for the marmalade to cool fully. Refrigerate for up to two weeks after transferring to a big, clean glass jar.

## 22. SWEET POTATO BREAKFAST BOWL

Serving: 2

Preparation time: 1 hr. 25 min

Nutritional values: Calories-356kcal|Carbs-58g|Protein-7g|Fat-12g

### Ingredients

- Sweet potato, 16 ounces (1 extremely large / 2 small)
- A pinch of cinnamon (to taste)
- 2 tbsp. raisins (optional)
- 2 tbsp. nuts, chopped
- Almond butter, 2 tbsp.

### Directions

- Preheat the oven to 375 degrees Fahrenheit. Sweet potatoes should be washed and gently dried. Wrap in aluminum foil after poking with a fork many times. Bake large sweet potatoes for 70 to 80 minutes, or tiny sweet potatoes for 60 to 65 minutes, or unless a fork easily protrudes the sweet potato. Allow for a minimum of five minutes of cooling time before peeling.
- Peel and gently mash cooled sweet potatoes with cinnamon as well as honey.
- If preferred, garnish with raisins, chopped nuts, as well as other toppings. Sprinkle with almond butter if eating straight away. If serving later, spread almond butter over the top right before dishing and reheating.

## 23. VEGAN GINGER BREAD SCONES WITH VANILLA BEAN GLAZE

Serving: 8

Preparation time: 31 min

Nutritional values: Calories-333kcal|Carbs-54g|Protein-6g|Fat-11g

### Ingredients

- 1 egg (flax)
- 2 cups of pastry flour (whole wheat)
- 1/2 cup + 2 tablespoons unsweetened almond milk 1/3 cup of coconut sugar
- molasses (1/3 cup)
- half vanilla beans

### Directions

- Preheat the oven to 400 degrees

Fahrenheit. Using parchment paper, line a baking sheet.

- Prepare the flax egg in a medium bowl. Allow for five min of resting time.

- Now, whisk together all of the dry ingredients in a large mixing bowl.

- After five min, pour the almond milk plus molasses into the flax egg. To thoroughly mix the ingredients, whisk them together. This will just take a minute or two! Place aside.

- Combine the dry ingredients with the hardened coconut oil. Mix the oil (coconut) into the mixture with a pastry cutter/fork unless the oil is the size of peas or similar.

- After that, gradually pour your wet components into the dry ingredients. Mix until everything is well mixed. It's alright if there's still some flour in the base of the bowl!

- Place the scone mixture on a baking sheet that has been lined with parchment paper. Make a 7-8-inch round out of the dough.

- Trim into 8 equal-sized slices using a sharp knife.

- Preheat oven to 350°F. Preheat oven to 350°F and bake for fourteen minutes.

- Sliced the scones twice (where you already cut) and take apart after fourteen minutes to allow the edges to bake.

- Bake for another 2 to 4 minutes (16-18 total). Alternatively, heat until lightly browned and well cooked.

- Allow 10 minutes for cooling.

- To prepare the glaze, whisk together all the ingredients (vanilla beans, sugar, and almond milk). In a mixing dish. Drizzle over the tops of the scones. To keep scones fresh, cover them completely. Enjoy.

## 24. PECAN PIE OVERNIGHT OATS

Serving: 6

Preparation time: 5 hr. 15 min

Nutritional values: Calories-292kcal|Carbs-28g|Protein-8g|Fat-16g

### Ingredients

- 2 tbsp. maple syrup
- 1 cup of diced pecans
- 1/4 tsp. of vanilla extract
- 2 cups of oats, old fashioned
- 2 cups of milk

### Directions

- Mix pecans, syrup (maple), brown sugar plus cinnamon, vanilla, as well as nutmeg in a medium pan and toast until thoroughly mixed, approximately 3 to 4

minutes; set aside.

- In a large mixing bowl, combine the oats, milk, & vanilla extract. Freeze for a minimum of five hours or overnight, covered.

- Serve the oats with the pecan mixture on top.

## 25. GINGER CORIANDER SPROUTED LENTILS AVOCADO TOAST

Serving: 3

Preparation time: 30 min

Nutritional values: Calories-424kcal|Carbs-44g|Protein-16g|Fat-22g

### Ingredients

- 3/4 cup dry lentils, 1.5 - 1.75 cup (288 g) seeded lentils

- 1/4 cup diced onion (40 g)
- 2 teaspoons ginger, chopped
- 1 medium tomato, finely sliced
- 3 - 4 slices of your favorite bread, gently toasted (optional)

## Directions

- Drench 3/4 cup of brown/green lentils overnight to sprout them. Remove soaking water and set aside. Put in a colander after washing and draining. Cover the colander openings with a clean towel or use a dish if the holes are too big. Allow standing on the counter, covered with a large wet cloth or a plate. Rinse twice a day, in the morning and evening. The lentils would sprout to a decent length in 2 to 3 days, based on the ambient temperature.

- Cook onion till transparent in ½ teaspoon oil or tablespoon water. 3 minutes Stir in the ginger. Cook for 30 seconds.

- Mix in the spices and a bit of salt. Cook for two minutes after adding the tomato. Larger chunks should be mashed.

- Mix in the sprouted lentils & salt. To heat completely, cover as well as cook for 2-3 minutes. Cover and heat for a minute after mixing and fluffing. Turn off the heat & cover for another 2 minutes to allow the flavors to blend.

- Place the mashed avocado over bread or toast to make the avocado toast. On avocado toast, serve the spicy lentils. Add sesame/hemp seeds, lemon, as well as pepper to taste. Warm the dish before serving.

## 26. SLOW COOKER STEEL CUT OATS WITH APPLE & CRANBERRIES

Serving: 4

Preparation time: 8 hr. 5 min

Nutritional values: Calories-285kcal|Carbs-50g|Protein-8g|Fat-6g

## Ingredients

- Bob's Red Mill Steel Sliced Oats, 1 cup (175 g)
- 1 apple, cored & sliced, Granny Smith
- 3 tbsp. maple syrup (pure)
- 1 tbsp. vanilla extract (pure)
- 4 1/2 cup of unsweetened almond milk (36 oz.) + extra for serving

## Directions

- Using cooking spray, gently coat a 2-quart to 4-quart slow cooker plate. The cooking liquid may evaporate more rapidly in slow cookers which run hot. This may cause a thicker skin/crust to form on the oats' surface or the edges of the insert. While in doubt, cut the cooking time in half and modify as needed.

- Mix in steel-cut oats, cranberries, maple syrup, and essence of vanilla, cinnamon, cardamom, as well as salt and milk (almond). To fully combine the ingredients, stir them together. Cook, covered, over low flame for six to eight hours (firmer oats) or longer (smoother oats with mild chew), turning once or twice if feasible. A thin, dark-colored skin may develop on the topping of the oats while they boil, making them seem somewhat dry at first sight. Don't be concerned. Stir the oats until they are frothy and smooth; the peel will be dissolved and integrated as a result of the stirring. Stir in an extra 12 cups or more of milk (almond) if you like looser oats. Serve immediately with preferred toppings.

## 27. STRAWBERRY BALSAMIC JAM

Serving: 1-2

Preparation time: 35 min

Nutritional values: Calories-92kcal|Carbs-23g|Protein-0.3g|Fat-0.1g

### Ingredients

- 1 lb. hulled & chopped strawberries
- 3 tbsp. sugar (or more to taste)
- 2 tbsp. balsamic vinegar (or more to flavor)

### Directions

- Mix strawberries, sugar, as well as balsamic vinegar in a large skillet to taste. Bring to a boil, then lower to medium heat and cook, stirring regularly, for 25-30 minutes, or until sauce has stiffened.

## 28. VEGAN FRENCH TOAST

Serving: 2-3

Preparation time: 15 min

Nutritional values: Calories-143kcal|Carbs-21g|Protein-8g|Fat-4g

### Ingredients

- 6 pieces day-old ciabatta bread, cut into 3/4-inch thick slices*
- Almond Breeze Almond Milk, 1 cup
- 1 tbsp. maple syrup, plus a little more for serving
- Millet flour (2 tbsp.)
- 1 tbsp. nutritional yeast

### Directions

- Mix the almond milk, syrup (maple), flour, yeast, cinnamon, nutmeg, as well as salt in a small mixing bowl.

- Arrange the bread in a small saucepan (with sides) large enough to contain it all. Pour the batter over the bread, carefully lift or toss it to ensure that all sides are covered evenly.

- In a large pan, heat a sprinkle of coconut oil over moderate flame. Add the bread pieces to the heated pan, then cook for a minute on each side until lightly browned.

- Serve with a sprinkling of powdered sugar, vegan butter, syrup of maple, as well as fresh fruit.

## 29. WHOLE WHEAT VEGAN WAFFLES

Serving: 8

Preparation time: 20 min

Nutritional values: Calories-340kcal|Carbs-37g|Protein-6g|Fat-20g

### Ingredients

- 1 1/2 cup room temperature pure Almond Milk,
- 1 1/2 tbsp. lemon juice
- 2 cups of whole wheat croissant flour (or white/wheat mixture) softly packaged
- 2 tbsp. flax meal (processed)
- 1/4 tsp. of cinnamon
- 2 tbsp. sugar from cane

### Directions

- Preheat the waffle iron.

- Blend Almond Breeze & juice of a lemon in a mixing bowl. Place aside.

- Mix all dry ingredients in a large mixing bowl (flour, 2 1/2 tsp. baking powder, processed flax meal, 1/2 tsp. cinnamon, cane sugar, & salt).

- Mix together the heated coconut oil plus vanilla in the small dish (containing the almond milk). Then, pour the wet components into the dry components and stir just until mixed (do not over mix).

- Brush a little spray for cooking on the waffle iron and pour in the mixture. For the perfect crunchy texture, cook for approximately one minute after the beeping.

- Enjoy waffles with butter, syrup (maple),

and fruit right away (while they're still hot!).

- Allow leftover waffles to cool before storing for speedy weekday waffles.

quired to keep the middles from burning.

- As desired, top with maple syrup, yogurt, as well as pecans.

## 30. PUMPKIN PANCAKES

Serving: 8

Preparation time: 28 min

Nutritional values: Calories-130kcal|Carbs-21g|Protein-4g|Fat-3g

### Ingredients

- 3 tbsp. water plus
- 1 tbsp. crushed flaxseed (or one egg)
- 2 tbsp. cane sugar 1 1/2 cup of all-purpose flour
- 1/2 cup of pumpkin puree (tinned)
- 1 cup + 3 tbsp. room temperature almond milk

### Directions

- Mix the flaxseed & water in a small saucepan and put aside for five min to settle.

- Mix together the flour, sugar (cane), baking powder plus soda, cinnamon, as well as salt in a large mixing bowl.

- Stir together the pureed pumpkin, almond milk, oil (coconut), vanilla, & flaxseed concoction in a medium mixing bowl.

- Transfer the wet components into the dry ingredients container and mix until everything is well blended. It's OK if there are a few blobs, but don't over-mix. The solution will be vicious, but if it is too thick, add a bit more almond milk gradually.

- Preheat a medium-hot non-stick pan or griddle. Spray the saucepan with coconut oil, then transfer the batter into it using a 1/3-cup measuring cup. Distribute the batter out a bit more using the base of the cup. Heat the pancakes for two minutes on each side, lowering the heat down as re-

## 31. CARROT WAFFLES

Serving: 4-6

Preparation time: 25 min

Nutritional values: Calories-240kcal|Carbs-34g|Protein-4g|Fat-10g

### Ingredients

- 2 cups of spelt flour (whole) or white/wheat mixture
- 2 tbsp. flaxseed, crushed
- Cinnamon (1/2 tsp.)
- 1 cup of shredded carrots
- 2 cups of room temperature almond milk

### Directions

- Heat up a waffle maker.

- Combine the flour, powder (baking), ground flaxseed, cinnamon, as well as a sprinkle of salt in a large mixing bowl.

- Combine the shredded carrots, milk (almond), oil (almond), vanilla, as well as maple syrup in a wide mixing bowl. Whisk in the carrot mix unless fully mixed with the dry ingredients.

- Scrape the batter into the waffle iron, then cook unless the sides are slightly crunchy. If using, drizzle with maple syrup & top with coconut cream.

## 32. TOFU SCRAMBLE

Serving: 4

Preparation time: 10 min

Nutritional values: Calories-121kcal|Carbs-10g|Protein-10g|Fat-5g

### Ingredients

- 1/3 cup of almond milk
- 2 chopped garlic cloves
- 1/2 tsp. mustard (Dijon)
- 1/2 cup yellow onion, chopped
- 1/4 oz. shredded extra-firm tofu, dried

### Directions

- Mix together the almond milk, yeast, chopped garlic, mustard, ground turmeric and cumin, as well as 1/2 tsp. salt in a small mixing bowl. Place aside.

- In a large frying pan, heat the oil (olive) over moderate flame. Cook, occasionally stirring, until the onion is tender, approximately 5 minutes. Sauté for 3 - 5 minutes, occasionally stirring, unless the tofu is fully cooked. Lower the heat and add the milk (almond) mixture, stirring constantly. Cook, stirring periodically, for 3 minutes. Sprinkle with more salt & freshly crushed black pepper to taste.

- If preferred, serve with vegetables, salsa, as well as tortillas.

## 33. AVOCADO TOAST

Serving: 2

Preparation time: 4 min

Nutritional values: Calories-237kcal|Carbs-21g|Protein-6g|Fat-15g

### Ingredients

- 1 avocado (ripe)
- For juicing, a lemon
- A pinch of sea salt
- 2 to 4 toasted slices of bread

### Directions

- Scrape the pit from the avocado and cut it in half vertically. While the avocado pulp is still within the peel, dice it with a tiny knife. Using a squash of lemon juice as well as a pinch of salt, season the pulp/flesh.

- Remove the chopped avocado flesh from the avocado peel and place it over the toasted bread. With the edge of a fork, pound the avocado, then garnish with your preferred toppings.

## 34. VEGAN CARROT LOX

Serving: 4

Preparation time: 40 min

Nutritional values: Calories-19kcal|Carbs-4g|Protein-0.7g|Fat-0.2g

### Ingredients

- 4 carrots, medium
- 3 tbsp. extra-virgin olive oil
- 1 tbsp. vinegar (rice)
- 1/2 tsp. paprika (smoked)
- Lemon juice, freshly squeezed

### Directions

- Preheat the oven at 475 degrees Fahrenheit and prepare a wide baking tray with parchment paper. Cover the base of the tray with a 1/4-inch layer of salt; next, add the carrots and a generous quantity of salt. Braise the carrots unless they are tender but not soggy when probed with a fork. The duration of time required will be determined by the size & quality of the carrots. Start checking them at 40 minutes. This step may be completed ahead of time.

- To prepare the marinade, follow these steps: Mix the extra-virgin olive oil, vinegar (rice), smoked paprika, lemon juice, as well as several pinches of freshly crushed black pepper in a casserole dish or small bowl.

- Allow the carrots to cool after removing them from the oven. Remove any extra salt with your hands. Slice a small strip from one edge of the salted skin with a knife, then strip the carrot into strands using a peeler. Toss the strands in the mixture to cover them. Place in the freezer for 15 to 30 min to marinate.

• End up serving with cream cheese, slices of cucumber, capers, chives, and/or dill on bagels.

• If you have any leftover carrots, cover and keep them in marinate in the refrigerator for up to four days

## 35. OATMEAL BREAKFAST COOKIES

Serving: 12

Preparation time: 30 min

Nutritional values: Calories-123kcal|Carbs-24g|Protein-4g|Fat-1g

### Ingredients

• 5 tbsp. warm water plus 2 tbsp. crushed flaxseed

• 1 cup of rolled oats, whole

• 1/2 c. almond flour

• 1 lemon zest (approximately 1/2 tsp.)

• 1/2 tsp. of cinnamon

• 1/2 cup of natural almond butter, smooth

### Directions

• Heat up the oven at 350 degrees Fahrenheit and prepare a wide baking tray with parchment paper.

• Blend the flaxseed & hot water in a small container and put aside to settle for five min.

• Combine the oat flour, one cup of rolled oats, almond flour, and zest of lemon, baking powder & soda, cinnamon, as well as salt in a large mixing bowl.

• Blend the almond butter, oil (coconut), plus maple syrup in a wide mixing bowl and whisk well to combine. Stir the flaxseed and water in a mixing bowl.

• Whisk the wet ingredients into the dry ingredients until they are evenly mixed. Combine the walnuts as well as blueberries in a mixing bowl.

• Scrape 1/4 cup of mixture onto the baking tray for each cookie. Bake for 20 - 24 min, or unless the sides are golden brown. Refrigerate for 5 - 10 min on the griddle before transferring to a cooling rack completely. The cookies may break apart if you remove them from the baking pan too soon.

• Cookies may be kept in a sealed jar or frozen once fully chilled.

## 36. MANGO COCONUT MUFFINS

Serving: 12

Preparation time: 30 min

Nutritional values: Calories-220kcal|Carbs-26g|Protein-4g|Fat-12g

### Ingredients

• 1 tbsp. flaxseed powder

• 2 tsp. lime juice, freshly squeezed

• 3/4 cup of ambient temperature almond milk

• 2 cups of spelt flour (or a mix of white and wheat flour)

• 1 cup of ripe mango, coarsely chopped

• 1/2 - 3/4 cup of coconut flakes, sugar-free

### Directions

• Preheat oven to 350 degrees Fahrenheit and prepare a 12-cup muffin pan with paper liners.

• Set aside to stiffen the crushed flaxseed plus water mixture. Set aside the almond milk after adding the lime juice.

- Mix the flour, powder for baking, salt, cinnamon, & 1/2 cup sugar in a large mixing bowl. Mix together the mixture of flaxseed, almond milk/lime juice combination, coconut oil, & vanilla in a wide mixing bowl.

- Add the wet components into the dry ingredients container and mix until everything is well blended. Do not over-mix the ingredients. Toss in the chopped mango and mix well.

- Distribute the mixture evenly between the muffins cups, topping them approximately three-quarters filled. Spread the coconut flakes on top, then bake for 15 - 20 min, or until a wooden skewer into the center pulls out clean. If necessary, finish with a little dusting of the remaining sugar. Allow cooling for ten min before transferring to a cooling rack to complete cooling.

## 37. VEGAN SCONES WITH RASPBERRIES

Serving: 12

Preparation time: 32 min

Nutritional values: Calories-194kcal|Carbs-14g|Protein-4g|Fat-14g

### Ingredients

- 3 cups of whole rolled oats (gluten-free)
- 1/2 cup of coconut flour 1/4 cup of cane sugar + 2 tbsp.
- 1 tbsp. powder of baking
- 1 cup of almond milk, chilled
- 2/3 cup of raspberries, halved

### Directions

- Preheat the oven at 400 degrees Fahrenheit and prepare a wide baking tray with parchment paper.

- To prepare the glaze, combine the powdered sugar & almond milk in a small dish. Place aside.

- Grind the oats into flour in a blender or food processor, then weigh out two level cups. Keep the rest of the flour for dusting.

- Combine the oat and coconut flour, sugar, powder of baking, as well as salt in a large mixing bowl. With the help of a pastry cutter or fork, cut in the cooled coconut oil unless the mixture resembles coarser pieces.

- Knead the dough lightly numerous times on a floured work surface, adding additional flour as required. Divide the dough into 2 equal portions. Stretch the dough down & put 1/3 cup of raspberries on 1 side of the dough, continuing with one part at a time. Spread the dough onto the berries, then gently press so that some berries peek through. Cut the dough into six triangles after shaping it into a 1" thick circle. Place the scones on the prepared baking sheet. Rep with the other half of the dough.

- Preheat oven to 350°F and bake for 12 - 15 minutes, or until lightly browned. Take the scones out from the oven and rest for ten min on the pan before placing them on a cooling rack altogether. Spread the glaze over them after they've cooled fully before serving,

## 38. OVERNIGHT OATS

Serving: 1

Preparation time: 5 min

Nutritional values: Calories-188kcal|Carbs-44g|Protein-10g|Fat-4g

### Ingredients

- 1/2 cup of rolled oats, whole
- 1/2 cup of almond milk / light coconut milk
- ½ tsp. of maple syrup
- A dash of salt
- Toppings of preference

### Directions

- Mix the oats, almond milk or coconut milk,

syrup (maple), as well as salt in a small container. Chill overnight after stirring.

- Spoon the oats into a plate in the morning and, if needed, add extra almond/coconut milk for thickness. Toppings may be added as desired.

- Alternatively, you may prepare the overnight oatmeal in bottles with the ingredients the night before for a fetch breakfast.

## 39. CINNAMON PECAN MUESLI

Serving: 8

Preparation time: 30 min

Nutritional values: Calories-413kcal|Carbs-51g|Protein-7g|Fat-18g

### Ingredients

- 1 cup of tart dry cherries
- 4 cups of oats, rolled
- 1 cup of large unsweetened flakes of coconut
- 1 1/2 cup of pecan chunks
- Vanilla extract (2 tsp.)

### Directions

- Heat up the oven at 350 degrees Fahrenheit.
- Put the dry cherries in a wide mixing bowl, then finely chop them.
- Distribute the oats out equally on a baking tray, then sprinkle the coconut on the upper side in an even quantity. Arrange the pecan pieces on a separate baking sheet. Bake for approximately 10 minutes unless the coconut is uniformly lightly browned on both trays, keeping an eye on them. Let the trays cool a bit after removing them from the oven.
- Mix the maple syrup as well as vanilla in a mixing bowl, then heat for 20 seconds in the microwave unless melted completely. Incorporate the roasted oats, coconut, & pecans with cherries, seasonings, & maple mixture in a large mixing bowl, then whisk to combine well. Return the mixture to the baking tray and roll it out evenly to enable it to dry completely approximately 10 minutes. Put to a canning jar after stirring to separate any clumps.

- Put milk over the top and sprinkle with maple syrup to garnish. The maple syrup provides the last touch of sweetness, so taste and adjust as needed. Freeze in a closed container or box; it thaws quickly, so there's no need to reheat.

## 40. NUTBUTTER TOAST

Serving: 8

Preparation time: 30 min

Nutritional values: Calories-103kcal|Carbs-4g|Protein-4g|Fat-9g

### Ingredients

- 2 cups of unprocessed nuts (or 1/3 cup each of almonds, cashews, as well as walnuts)
- To taste kosher salt
- As needed, grapeseed/canola oil (1 tbsp.)
- Roasted coconut is an optional ingredient.

### Directions

- Heat up the oven to 325 degrees Fahrenheit.
- Using a rimmed baking sheet, distribute the nuts out. For 20 - 25 min, toast until aromatic and toasted. Allow 2 - 3 minutes for cooling on the tray.
- While still heated, put to food processor & process for 4 - 12 minutes, cleaning the sides as needed. If the nuts are extremely dry and grainy after several minutes, add up to a tbsp. of oil during processing.
- When the mixture is smooth, season with kosher salt as per taste (1/4 tsp. for unsalted nuts), transfer the butter to a container and keep it in the fridge for up to four weeks.

# 41. BANANA BAKED OATMEAL

Serving: 6 - 8

Preparation time: 45 min

Nutritional values: Calories-243kcal|Carbs-37g|Protein-5g|Fat-7g

## Ingredients

- Rolled oats, 2 cups
- 1 1/2 tsp. cinnamon
- Allspice (1/2 tsp.)
- 2 extremely ripe bananas (3/4 cup squished banana)
- 1 3/4 cups of milk (dairy/ almond/oat)

## Directions

- Preheat oven at 375°F.

- Use coconut oil or even a mild oil to coat an 8 x 8" or 9 × 9" pan. Toss the rolled oats, pieces of pecan, powder (baking), cinnamon, allspice, as well as kosher salt together in a large mixing bowl.

- Place the dried products in the pan that has been prepared.

- The bananas should be mashed. Combine the bananas, milk, syrup (maple), and vanilla in the same mixing bowl to combine. Over the oats, pour the milk batter. To make sure everything is evenly combined, gently stir with a fork.

- Bake for 40-45 minutes, or until the oat batter has settled and the top is beautifully brown. Give at least 10 to 15 minutes for cooling after removing from the oven.

- Spread almond butter, either peanut butter (or even a mix of the two) over the center before serving, then top with sliced bananas.

# 42. ACAI BOWL

Serving: 2

Preparation time: 15 min

Nutritional values: Calories-411kcal|Carbs-71g|Protein-9g|Fat-14g

## Ingredients

- 1 cup of pineapple cubes, frozen
- 1 banana, medium
- 1/2 mango (or 1/2 cup chopped iced mango)
- 1 tbsp. lime juice
- 7 oz. chilled sugar - free acai puree (like Sambazon)

## Directions

- Put the bowls in the refrigerator to prevent the acai from liquefying while you're eating it.

- To avoid melting, prepare the toppings (again, before creating the bowl): Sauté the coconut in a shallow saucepan over low to moderate low flame until lightly browned, turning often. Remove to a dish right away. Half of the mango should be set aside for the acai. Strawberries should be sliced.

- Process the pineapple, banana, as well as mango in a large, high-powered or normal blender until well mixed and gritty.

- Remove the package and thaw the acai puree in warm water so it can be split into smaller pieces. In a blender, combine the acai, lime juice, as well as 1/4 cup ice water. Stop and whisk as needed until the mixture is smooth. (If you need additional water, add it, but don't add too much since you want the acai consistency to be thick.) A high-powered blender will work nicely here; a normal blender will need more stopping and stirring.)

- Fill the chilled bowls with the acai concoction. Serve with the fruits, coconut, pepitas, and any desired toppings. Serve right away.

# 43. VEGAN BLUEBERRY PANCAKES

Serving: 8

Preparation time: 20 min

Nutritional values: Calories-116kcal|Carbs-18g|Protein-2g|Fat-4g

## Ingredients

- 1 egg (flax)
- 1 cup of flour, all-purpose
- 1 cup of almond milk
- Apple cider vinegar, 1 tsp.
- 1 cup of blueberries (fresh or frozen)

## Directions

- Start making the (flax) egg (it needs to settle for fifteen minutes).

- Next, stir together the all-purpose flour, powder (baking), cinnamon, as well as kosher salt in a large mixing bowl.

- Pour the almond milk, vinegar (apple cider), maple syrup, & oil into a large bowl. Add the egg once it has finished cooking.

- Combine the wet and dry ingredients in a mixing bowl. If desired, a bit of turmeric may be added.

- Using more grapeseed/vegetable oil, gently brush a skillet. Warm the skillet over medium-high heat. Put blueberries on top of the batter in tiny rounds. Fry the pancakes unless the tops bubble and the bases are nicely browned. Then turn them and continue to cook until they're done.

- Eat with maple syrup right away.

# 44. APPLE CINNAMON STEEL CUT OATS

Serving: 8-10

Preparation time: 30 min

Nutritional values: Calories-360kcal|Carbs-57g|Protein-11g|Fat-11g

## Ingredients

- Three apples
- Millville steel-cut oats, 3 cups
- 8 cups of water
- Vanilla extract (two tsp.)
- 2 tsp. cinnamon powder

## Directions

- Cut the apples by coring them and slicing them thinly, then chopping the pieces into bite-sized chunks. In a pressure cooker, combine the apples, oats (steel cut), water, extract of vanilla, cinnamon, as well as salt. Close the lid. Put the "Sealing" setting on the pressure relief handle.

- Cook for four minutes on increased pressure: Set the timer for four minutes on the Pressure Cook setting. The pot must "preheat" and "bring up to pressure" for approximately 10 minutes before it can begin cooking. Wait for the oats to finish cooking.

- For ten min, wait for natural release: Wait ten min after the pressure cooker sounds to enable the pressure cooker to automatically release pressure. After ten min, turn the vent to "Venting" & cover the hand with a cloth or hot pad to release any residual steam.

- To get a creamy consistency, lift the lid, then stir. Serve with a drizzle of syrup (maple), milk, diced apples, as well as cashew butter on the side. Keep leftovers in the fridge for up to five days.

## 45. ORANGE & MINT SALAD

Serving: 4

Preparation time: 15 min

Nutritional values: Calories-222kcal|Carbs-54g|Protein-4g|Fat-1g

### Ingredients

- Four oranges
- 12 dates, stoned and sliced lengthwise
- A tiny bunch of mint, finely diced leaves with a few leaves left intact
- 1 tablespoon rosewater/rose syrup

### Directions

- Remove the white pith from the oranges while peeling and segmenting them. Place in a dish with any juices, then mix gently with the dates, chopped mint, as well as rose syrup. Serve by dividing the mixture among four dessert dishes and scattering the mint leaves on top.

## 46. PISTACHIO & CARDAMOM BUTTER

Serving: 1

Preparation time: 25 min

Nutritional values: Calories-87kcal|Carbs-3g|Protein-3g|Fat-7g

### Ingredients

- Ten pods of cardamom
- Pistachio nut kernels (400g)
- 1 tablespoon of maple syrup
- 1/2 teaspoon flakes of sea salt
- 2–3 teaspoon groundnut oil

### Directions

- Take out the seeds of cardamom from the pods, then smash them coarsely in a mortar & pestle.
- In a stick blender, combine the nuts, ground cardamom, maple syrup, as well as salt. Blend for 7-8 minutes, or until you get creamy butter; if the consistency is too thick, pour in more oil and blend again.

## 47. THREE-GRAIN PORRIDGE

Serving: 18

Preparation time: 10 min

Nutritional values: Calories-179kcal|Carbs-32g|Protein-7g|Fat-2g

### Ingredients

- Oatmeal, 300g
- Spelt flakes (300g)
- 300 g flakes of barley
- To serve, agave syrup & chopped strawberries (optional)

### Directions

- In a wide, dry frying pan, roast the oats, spelt flakes, as well as barley in sections for 5 minutes until brown, then cool & keep in a sealed jar.
- Simply mix 50 grams of the porridge batter with 300ml milk/water in a skillet when ready to eat. Cook for 5 minutes, stirring periodically, then sprinkle with honey and garnish with strawberries, if desired (optional).

## 48. VEGAN BANANA & WALNUT BREAD

Serving: 8

Preparation time: 1 hr.

Nutritional values: Calories-315kcal|Carbs-38g|Protein-6g|Fat-15g

## Ingredients

- Almonds, ground, 25g
- 75 g sugar, mild muscovado
- 4 dates, diced finely
- Mash bananas, 3-4 extremely ripe bananas
- 75g roasted walnut pieces

## Directions

- Preheat oven at 200°C/180°C fan/gas. Line a 450g loaf pan with baking paper after brushing it with some oil.

- Combine the flour, almonds, powder (baking), sugar, as well as dates in a large mixing bowl. Mix the pureed banana & oil in a mixing bowl, then stir in the mixture of flour. To soften the mixture, apply the soya milk, stir in the walnuts, and then scoop the batter into the tin. Bake for 1 hour, wrapping the top with foil if it begins to brown too much. In the middle of the cake, introduce a skewer, and it should pull out clean. Transfer to the oven & cook for another 10 minutes if necessary. Allow cooling for 15 minutes before removing from the tin.

## 49. BLACKCURRANT COMPOTE

Serving: 1

Preparation time: 20 min

Nutritional values: Calories-15kcal|Carbs-3g|Protein-0g|Fat-0g

## Ingredients

- 1/2 lemon juice
- Blackcurrants (500g)
- 100 g of caster sugar (golden)

## Directions

- In a wide skillet, put 2 tablespoons of water as well as the lemon juice to a simmer, then include the blackcurrants & cook until they are broken down.

- Using a temperature probe, heat the caster sugar (golden) to 105°C. Allow cooling before pouring into sterilized jars.

## 50. BREAKFAST NAAN

Serving: 2

Preparation time: 10 min

Nutritional values: Calories-503kcal|Carbs-35g|Protein-20g|Fat-30g

## Ingredients

- Two eggs
- 2 naan bread, medium
- 4 tablespoons cream cheese (low-fat)
- Mango chutney, 2 tablespoons
- 1 halved & diced avocado

## Directions

- Preheat the oven at 200°C/180°C. In a skillet, heat the oil and then cook the eggs. Although the eggs are cooking, heat the bread (naan) in the oven.

- Sprinkle the chutney over the heated naans after spreading cream cheese on them. Sprinkle each naan with a poached egg and the avocado, lemon, chili, & coriander. Season to taste and serve.

## 51. PEANUT BUTTER & BANANA OVERNIGHT OATS

Serving: 1

Preparation time: 8 hr. 5 min

Nutritional values: Calories-297kcal|Carbs-50g|Protein-8g|Fat-9g

## Ingredients

- 1/2 cup of rolled oats, old-fashioned
- 1 cup of almond milk (unsweetened)
- 1 tablespoon of chia seeds
- 1/2 banana, ripe and sliced
- 1 tablespoon of peanut butter

## Directions

- Mix the oats, sugar-free almond milk, as well as chia seeds in a mixing bowl. Stir in the sprinkle of vanilla once everything has come together.

- Place plastic wrap/cling film around the bowl. Refrigerate for at least one night to cool.

- Spoon the peanut butter & diced banana in a medium microwave-safe dish the following day. Heat for 10-20 seconds on medium, or unless the bananas are mushy and also the peanut butter begins to melt.

- Distribute the pecans on a baking tray to toast. Bake for 5 to 8 minutes around 350°F/180°C, or until aromatic. Pecans have a tendency to burn fast, so pay attention to them.

- Take the oats out of the fridge and discard the plastic wrap. Top with the banana & peanut mixture.

- Pecans, as well as maple syrup, are sprinkled on top. Serve immediately and enjoy.

# 52. EASY CANNED PEACHES

Serving: 8

Preparation time: 1 hr.

Nutritional values: Calories-50kcal|Carbs-12g|Protein-0g|Fat-0g

## Ingredients

- 20 large ripe peaches
- 3 cups of sugar (granulated)
- 6 cups of water
- 8 pints of jars

## Directions

- We'll start by paring the peaches, but we'll employ a small technique to make the process go more smoothly. Begin by boiling a wide pot of water and preparing an ice bucket nearby.

- Each peach should have an X carved into the base.

- Place 4 - 5 peaches in the water at a time and let simmer for approximately 1 minute. Don't overcook the peaches; instead, steam them until the peel begins to strip away from the pulp.

- Take the peaches out from the hot water with a wide slotted spoon & place them in the improvised ice bucket.

- After you've stunned them all in the ice, scrape them using the etched X as a guide. Split them into halves and discard the pit after you've skinned all of them. They should be quartered.

- Fill your containers with whatever flavorings you like (cinnamon, vanilla, etc.) and start putting the sliced peaches in the containers, crater down. This is crucial because it enables you to put several peaches into the container with the hole facing down. Allow approximately a 12-inch margin between both the top of the peaches as well as the jar top.

- Melt the sugar & water to prepare the syrup; meanwhile, you fill the jars.

- Carefully pour the hot syrup mixture into the jars after all of the peaches have been packed into them. Slowing down will enable the mixture to seep into the peaches.

- Cover the jars and place as many as possible in a canner. Process for approximately half an hour.

- Serve and have fun.

## 53. FLAXSEED BLUEBERRY OATMEAL

Serving: 2

Preparation time: 10 min

Nutritional values: Calories-374kcal|Carbs-48g|Protein-11g|Fat-13g

### Ingredients

- 1 cup of oats, rolled
- 2 tablespoons toasted pecans, finely diced
- 2 tablespoons flaxseed, ground
- 1/3 cup of blueberries
- 1 tablespoon honey
- 1 cup of milk

### Directions

- In a medium saucepan, whisk the milk & water, then bring to a simmer over moderate flame. Turn down the heat to moderate after it achieves boiling point.

- Combine the oats, ground flaxseed, as well as salt in a mixing bowl. Cook, often stirring, for five min, or until the oats begin to stiffen.

- Turn off the heat in the saucepan. Allow sitting for two min after covering with a dishcloth.

- Stir the oats a few times before dividing them into two bowls. Spritz with honey and garnish with blueberries, pecans, & nuts. Enjoy.

## 54. CHIA PEANUTBUTTER OATS

Serving: 1

Preparation time: 12 hr.

Nutritional values: Calories-316kcal|Carbs-37g|Protein-11g|Fat-14g

### Ingredients

- 3/4 cup of oats, rolled
- Chia seeds (2 tbsp.)
- 1 cup of vanilla almond milk (or some other plant milk)*, unsweetened
- 1 ripe banana, melded (leaving few banana pieces for garnish!)
- 1 1/2 tbsp. water + tbsp. PB Fit powder (or some other nut butter, as per taste)

### Directions

- In a small container, combine the oats, chia seeds, cinnamon, as well as sea salt. Combine almond milk, water, vanilla, plus pureed banana in a mixing bowl. Stir until everything is well mixed.

- Combine the powder of PB with water in a medium bowl until smooth. You may increase the amount of peanut butter taste by doubling the components. Fill Mason jar halfway with "peanut butter" concoction. Toppings may be added both now and in the morning!

- Refrigerate for at least 3 - 4 hours or overnight. Using a spoon, dip in and enjoy.

## 55. SCRAMBLED TOFU BREAKFAST BURRITO

Serving: 4

Preparation time: 30 min

Nutritional values: Calories-316kcal|Carbs-37g|Protein-11g|Fat-14g

### Ingredients

- 1 packet medium or extra-firm tofu (12 oz.)
- 3 garlic cloves (minced) & 1 tablespoon hummus
- 5 baby potatoes, whole (diced into bite-size chunks)
- 1 red bell pepper, large (thinly sliced)

- 2 cups of kale, diced

## Directions

- Preheat the oven at 400 degrees Fahrenheit (204 degrees Celsius) and prepare a baking tray with parchment paper. Meanwhile, cover the tofu in a damp towel and place anything hefty on top of it, like a cast-iron pan, to push out any extra liquid. Then, using a fork, break into tiny pieces. Place aside.

- Toss the potatoes & red pepper with the oil (or water) as well as seasonings on the baking sheet to mix. Cook for 15-22 minutes, or until fork soft and golden brown. Incorporate the kale with the other veggies and spices in the final five min of baking to turn it brown.

- Meanwhile, preheat a wide skillet over medium-high heat. When the pan is heated, add the oil (or water), chopped garlic, as well as tofu and cook, turning regularly, for 7 to 10 minutes, until the tofu is slightly browned.

- Meanwhile, combine the hummus, chili powder, ground cumin, nutritional yeast, sea salt, & cayenne in a medium mixing bowl (optional). To mix, stir everything together. Next, add water unless a spreadable sauce develops. Then toss in the parsley. Sauté the tofu with the spice blend until it is nicely browned, about 3-5 minutes over moderate flame. Place aside.

- Make the burritos as follows: A wide tortilla should be rolled out. Serve with roasted veggies, scrambled tofu, diced avocado, cilantro, as well as a drizzle of salsa. Roll it up and put it seam side down. Continue unless you've used up all of the toppings, which should be approximately 3-4 large burritos.

- To get the best results, eat it right away. You may also wrap and refrigerate them for up to four days.

## 56. SEEDY HUMMUS TOAST

Serving: 1

Preparation time: 8 min

Nutritional values: Calories-316kcal|Carbs-24g|Protein-19g|Fat-16g

## Ingredients

- 2 sprouted wheat bread pieces
- 1/4 cup of hummus
- Hemp seeds, a tablespoon
- 1 tablespoon unsalted toasted sunflower seeds

## Directions

- Make the bread toasty. Then add hummus, 1/4 cup of hemp seeds, as well as sunflower seeds on the top! Eat it right away.

## 57. GREEK CHICKPEAS ON TOAST

Serving: 2

Preparation time: 30 min

Nutritional values: Calories-510kcal|Carbs-45g|Protein-22g|Fat-15g

## Ingredients

- 3 thinly chopped shallots
- 2 finely chopped garlic cloves
- 2 large tomatoes alternatively 1 × 400 g stripped plum tomato can
- 2 cups of chickpeas (cooked)
- 4-6 heated crusty bread pieces (gluten-free if needed)

## Directions

- In a large pan, heat the olive oil.

- Toss in the shallots and cook until they are nearly transparent about 5 minutes. Sauté until the shallots are fully transparent and the garlic has softened, then add the garlic.

- In a pan, combine all of the spices. Toss

them in with the garlic and onions and cook for 1-2 min, stirring constantly.

- While adding canned tomatoes to the saucepan with a few tbsp. of water, squish them or dice them coarsely. Boil until the gravy has thickened over moderate flame.

- Sauté the chickpeas in the sauce until they are warmed through. Add salt, sugar, as well as black pepper to taste.

- With a sprinkling of fresh herbs as well as some black olives, served on crusty bread.

## 58. ALMOND MILK & CHAI QUINOA BOWL

Serving: 1

Preparation time: 25 min

Nutritional values: Calories-482kcal|Carbs-48g|Protein-12g|Fat-10g

### Ingredients

- 1/2 cup of washed quinoa
- 1 chai tea bag 1 cup of unsweetened almond milk
- Optional: 1/2 tablespoon coconut palm sugar
- Cinnamon

### Directions

- Rinse the quinoa thoroughly before cooking. This negates saponin (quinoa's natural covering), which may cause the taste bitter.

- Bring almond milk, washed quinoa, as well as the chai tea bag to a simmer in a medium saucepan. Discard the chai (tea bag) after the almond milk has reached a boil. Stir in the coconut sugar (if using). Turn down the heat to a low simmer, then cook the quinoa for approximately 15 to 20 minutes, covered.

- Take the quinoa out from the heat & cover for a further 5-10 minutes to allow the almond milk to soak completely.

- To serve, combine the quinoa with a little extra hot milk in a dish. The pecan plus walnut milk would also be fantastic! Serve with nuts, coconut, and a pinch of cinnamon on top.

## 59. SPICY SCRAMBLED TOFU BREAKFAST TACOS

Serving: 3

Preparation time: 30 min

Nutritional values: Calories-260kcal|Carbs-30g|Protein-13g|Fat-9g

### Ingredients

- 1 cored & chopped poblano pepper
- 1/2 large chopped red onion
- 3 Roma tomatoes
- 1 large diced roasted red bell pepper from a jar (approximately 1/2 cup)
- 1 (16-oz.) block firm or extra-firm seeded tofu, washed and drained

### Directions

- Warm the olive oil in a large frying pan over moderate heat. Fry for 4 - 6 min, or unless the poblano pepper, as well as red onion, start to soften, stirring periodically.

- Next, whirl the Roma tomatoes multiple times in a processor to crush and purée them. Place aside.

- Toss the pepper as well as onion combination with the roasted red pepper, chili powder, paprika (smoked), & sea salt. Proceed to sauté for another minute, or unless the flavors have bloomed and are aromatic.

- Toss in the diced Roma tomatoes and tofu crumbles. Cook, stirring periodically, for 10 to 12 min, or unless the liquid has reduced.

- Continue to cook for another minute after

adding the lime juice. Now turn the heat off.

- If desired, sprinkle with more sea salt.

- Scoop a little amount of tofu mixture into each heated tortilla to serve. Top with a spoonful of avocado (mashed), a sprinkling of cilantro, and a few splashes of hot sauce, if desired (if using).

- Serve right away.

- Leftovers may be stored in different containers in the refrigerator for up to two days.

## 60. FLUFFY VEGAN PROTEIN PANCAKES

Serving: 2

Preparation time: 10 min

Nutritional values: Calories-295kcal|Carbs-60g|Protein-16g|Fat-1g

### Ingredients

- 1 cup of all-purpose flour (120 g)
- 1/4 cup of (28 g) preferred vegan protein powder
- 1 tablespoon of baking powder
- 2 tablespoons maple syrup
- 1 cup of water, + more water as required

### Directions

- In a mixing bowl, combine the flour, vegan protein powder, baking powder, as well as salt.

- If using, drizzle in the syrup (maple) or flavor of choice, then gently drizzle in the water, stirring until "evenly mixed." It ought to be chunky and viscous but not too thick to pour. If necessary, add a bit more water.

- Whilst batter rests, preheat a pan at low to moderate heat. For each pancake, coat the pan with cooking spray or use a nice non-stick pan. Spread approximately 1/4 cup of batter into the pan.

- Fry until bubbles form around the sides of each pancake as well as the edges seem dry & firm. Cook for another 1-2 minutes on the other side.

- Serve with your favorite pancake toppings right away. Leftovers may be kept refrigerated or frozen and warmed as required.

## 61. SIMPLE VEGAN OMELET

Serving: 2

Preparation time: 10 min

Nutritional values: Calories-232kcal|Carbs-22g|Protein-22g|Fat-8g

### Ingredients

- 5 oz. solid silken tofu (washed & patted dry / 5 oz. makes 3/4 cup)
- 2 tablespoons hummus
- Two large garlic cloves (chopped)
- 2 tablespoons yeast (nutritional)
- 1 cup of vegetables of your choice

### Directions

- Preheat the oven at 375 degrees Fahrenheit (190 C).

- Prepare the vegetables, rinse and dry the tofu, then chop the garlic cloves. Place aside.

- Over moderate flame, warm a medium oven-safe saucepan. When the pan is heated, add the olive oil & garlic and sauté for 1-2 minutes, or until the garlic is slightly golden brown.

- Put garlic to a stick blender with the rest of the omelet ingredients (tofu, cornstarch) & process until smooth, scraping down the sides as required. To thin, use no more than 1-2 tablespoons of water. Place aside.

- Add a little extra olive oil as well as the vegetables to the still-warm pan over moderate heat. Sprinkle with salt & pepper and cook until done to your taste. To give each ingredient enough time to simmer, start with onions & tomatoes, next include mushrooms, and last spinach. Place aside.

- Take the skillet off from the heat & cover it with enough oil to prevent the omelet from sticking. Return 1/4 of the vegetables to the pan and pour on the omelet batter, distributing it carefully with a fork or rubber spatula to avoid tearing or gaps. The more uniformly and thinly you can distribute it, the better. As a result, you may not be able to use it all.

- Fry for 5 minutes on the moderate flame on the stovetop or until the sides begin to dry. Put in oven & bake for 10-15 minutes, or until dry and nicely browned. The more it bakes, the less smooth it becomes, so if you want a more "well-cooked" omelet, cook it for 15 minutes or longer.

## 62. CINNAMON ROLL OVERNIGHT OATS

Serving: 5

Preparation time: 8 hr.

Nutritional values: Calories-197kcal|Carbs-34g|Protein-5g|Fat-4g

### Ingredients

- 2 1/2 cups of rolled oats, old-fashioned
- 2 1/2 cups of unsweetened dairy-free milk (almond, coconut, etc.)
- 8 tsp. brown sugar (mild)
- 2 1/2 tsp. vanilla extract
- 1 1/4 tsp. cinnamon powder

### Directions

- In a large mixing bowl, combine the oats, unsweetened milk, and 8 tsp. brown sugar, extract of vanilla, cinnamon, & salt. Divide the mixture into five 8 oz. jars. Chill in the fridge or for up to five days after screwing on the lids.

## 63. EVERYTHING BAGEL AVOCADO TOAST

Serving: 1

Preparation time: 5 min

Nutritional values: Calories-172kcal|Carbs-17g|Protein-5g|Fat-10g

### Ingredients

- 1/4 large mashed avocado
- 2 tablespoons everything bagel seasoning
- 1 piece whole-grain bread, toasted
- 1 tsp. granular sea salt (like Maldon)

### Directions

- On the toast, spread avocado. Sprinkle with salt & pepper

## 64. QUICK-COOKING OATS

Serving: 1

Preparation time: 5 min

Nutritional values: Calories-150kcal|Carbs-27g|Protein-5g|Fat-3g

### Ingredients

- 1 cup of low-fat milk or water
- 1 teaspoon of salt
- 1/2 cup of oats (quick-cooking)
- 1 oz. fluid for serving, use low-fat milk.
- 1 tsp. For serving, 1 to 2 tsp. honey, cane sugar, preferably brown sugar

### Directions

- In a medium saucepan, mix water (or milk) as well as salt. Bring the water to a boil. Turn down the heat and stir in the oats; cook for one minute. Take the pan off the heat, cover, and set aside for

2 - 3 min.

• In a 2-cup oven-safe bowl, mix water (or milk), salt, plus oats. Heat for 1 to 2 min on maximum. Before serving, give it a good stir.

• Serve with milk, honey, cinnamon, dry fruits, as well as nuts, if desired.

## 65. PEANUTBUTTER BANANA CINNAMON TOAST

Serving: 1

Preparation time: 5 min

Nutritional values: Calories-266kcal|Carbs-38g|Protein-8g|Fat-9g

### Ingredients

- 1 toasted whole-wheat bread slice
- Peanut butter, 1 tbsp.
- 1 tiny chopped banana
- To taste cinnamon

### Directions

• Sprinkle peanut butter on the bread, then top with sliced bananas. To taste, add a little cinnamon.

## 66. WHITE BEAN & AVOCADO TOAST

Serving: 1

Preparation time: 5 min

Nutritional values: Calories-230kcal|Carbs-34g|Protein-11g|Fat-8g

### Ingredients

- 1 toasted whole-wheat bread slice
- 1/4 smashed avocado
- 1/2 cup washed and drained can of white beans

• Season with freshly cracked black pepper to taste

• 1 tsp. red pepper, crushed

### Directions

• Add mashed avocado as well as white beans to the toast. Add a bit of salt, pepper, & cracked red pepper to taste.

## 67. VEGAN PUMPKIN BREAD

Serving: 12

Preparation time: 2 hr. 20 min

Nutritional values: Calories-191kcal|Carbs-30g|Protein-3g|Fat-7g

### Ingredients

- Flaxseed meal, 2 tbsp.
- 3/4 cup of almond milk, unsweetened
- Sugar (3/4 cup)
- 1/2 cup of pumpkin puree (unseasoned)
- 1 tsp. cinnamon/pumpkin pie spice

### Directions

• Preheat the oven at 350 degrees Fahrenheit. Using cooking spray, spray a 9x5-inch bread pan.

• In a small dish, mix water as well as a flaxseed meal. Let it rest for several minutes.

• In a medium mixing bowl, combine the almond milk, 3/4 cup of sugar, oil, extract of vanilla, as well as flaxseed mixture. Add the pumpkin puree and mix well. In a large mixing bowl, combine flour, powder of baking, pumpkin pie seasoning (or cinnamon), and salt. Mix in the wet ingredients unless just mixed. If using, toss in chocolate chips. Place the batter in the pan that has been prepared.

• Bake for 1 hr. - 1 hr. 15 min, or until brown

and a toothpick injected in the middle comes out clean. Refrigerate for ten min in the pan before turning out onto a wire rack to cool completely. Allow 1 hour to cool before slicing.

## 68. OLD-FASHIONED OATMEAL

Serving: 1

Preparation time: 15 min

Nutritional values: Calories-150kcal|Carbs-27g|Protein-5g|Fat-3g

### Ingredients

- 1 cup of low-fat milk/water
- 1/2 cup of oats, rolled
- 1 oz. liquid for serving, use low-fat milk.
- 1 tsp. For serving, 1 to 2 tbsp. honey, cane sugar, as well as brown sugar
- 1 pinch of cinnamon

### Directions

- In a medium saucepan, mix water (preferably milk) as well as salt. Bring the water to a boil. Turn down the heat and whisk in oats; cook for 5 min, stirring periodically. Take the pan off the heat, cover, and set aside for 2 - 3 min.

- In a 2-cup heat-safe bowl, mix water (preferably milk), salt, as well as oats. Microwave for 2 1/2 - 3 min on maximum. Before serving, give it a good stir.

- If preferred, serve with milk, sweetener, a pinch of cinnamon, dry fruits, or nuts.

## 69. APPLE CINNAMON OVERNIGHT OATS

Serving: 1

Preparation time: 6 hr.

Nutritional values: Calories-215kcal|Carbs-45g|Protein-5g|Fat-4g

### Ingredients

- 1/2 cup of rolled oats, old-fashioned
- 1/2 cup of almond milk, unsweetened
- 1/4 tsp. ground cinnamon
- 1 tsp. maple syrup
- 1/2 cup apple, chopped

### Directions

- In a pint-sized container, mix together the oats, milk (almond), seeds of chia (if using), syrup (maple), cinnamon, as well as salt. Chill overnight, covered.

- If preferred, garnish with an apple as well as pecans before serving.

## 70. BLUEBERRY BANANA OVERNIGHT OATS

Serving: 1

Preparation time: 6 hr.

Nutritional values: Calories-285kcal|Carbs-56g|Protein-6g|Fat-5g

### Ingredients

- 1/2 cup of coconut milk beverage (unsweetened)
- 1/2 cup of oats, old-fashioned
- 1/2 mashed banana
- 1 tsp. of maple syrup
- 1/2 cup blueberries, fresh

### Directions

- In a pint-sized container, whisk together coconut milk, old-fashioned oats, and seeds of chia, mashed banana, syrup (maple), and salt. If preferred, top with blueberries as well as coconut. Chill overnight, covered.

- Enjoy the next morning.

# CHAPTER 3: VEGAN DRINKS AND SMOOTHIES

## 1. BLACK CHERRY BOURBON COLA SMASH

Serving: 2

Preparation time: 5 min

Nutritional values: Calories-240kcal|Carbs-19g|Protein-0g|Fat-0g

### Ingredients

- 6 sliced ripe black cherries
- Bourbon, 2 oz.
- 1-ounce cherry brandy
- ½ a lime juice + slices to serve
- Topping up with chilled cola, ginger beer, and soda water

### Directions

- In a cocktail shaker, combine the cherries, 2 oz. Bourbon, cherry brandy, and lime juice. Using a jumbling spoon or the point of a rolling pin, smash the cherries.
- Whisk for thirty seconds with ice in the cocktail shaker.
- Add lots of ice to two rocks glasses. Divide the drink amongst the glasses after straining it over the ice.
- Top with cola & garnish with a slice of lime. Serve right away.

## 2. PINK DRINK

Serving: 4

Preparation time: 25 min

Nutritional values: Calories-55kcal|Carbs-10g|Protein-0g|Fat-2g

### Ingredients

- 1 teabag of hibiscus
- 1 tbsp. maple syrup/honey
- 8 strawberries (ripe), halved, hulled & finely diced
- 1/2 cup of freshly squeezed orange juice
- 1/2 cup of coconut milk (light) (can/carton)

### Directions

- Bring water to a low boil, then reduce to low heat. In a 1-quart (4-cup) fluid measuring cup or medium heat-resistant pitcher, put the teabag. Pour the hot water across the tea bag, whisk in the honey unless it's completely dissolved, then add half of the diced strawberries. Allow 10 to 20 min for the solution to settle.
- Remove the teabag and throw it away. Stir in the orange juice & coconut milk until everything is well combined. Fill glasses halfway with ice, then distribute the pink cocktail among them. Add the rest sliced strawberries to the glasses as a garnish. Serve right away.

## 3. GINGER BEER MOJITO

Serving: 1

Preparation time: 1 min

Nutritional values: Calories-275kcal|Carbs-45g|Protein-4g|Fat-1g

### Ingredients

- 10 leaves of mint
- 2 oz. lime juice (fresh) ice
- 1.5 oz. rum (light)
- Ginger beer, 4 oz.
- Garnishes: mint sprigs, lime or lemon wedges or chunks

### Directions

- In a glass, crush the mint with the lime juice. Stir in the rum & ginger beer once a few huge ice cubes have been added. If preferred, garnish the cocktail with extra garnishes.

## 4. FROZEN BLACKBERRY COOLERS

Serving: 2

Preparation time: 5 min

Nutritional values: Calories-157kcal|Carbs-14g|Protein-19g|Fat-4g

### Ingredients

- 3 cups blackberries, chilled
- Coconut milk (1/2 cup)
- Lime juice (two tbsp.)
- Simple syrup, 1/4 cup
- 6 oz. of rum

### Directions

- Blend chilled blackberries, cubes of ice, half cup of coconut milk, juice of lime, simple syrup, as well, as rum together unless smooth & pureed. If you're using fresh blackberries, add additional ice until the mixture is completely frozen. To increase the sweetness, add extra simple syrup. Serve with blackberries as well as a bunch of mint as a garnish.

## 5. STRAWBERRY PEACH ICED TEA

Serving: 7

Preparation time: 50 min

Nutritional values: Calories-127kcal|Carbs-31g|Protein-0g|Fat-0g

### Ingredients

- 2 finely diced large ripe peaches
- 1 cup of hulled and coarsely chopped fresh strawberries
- Sugar (1 cup)
- 2 tea bags (black or green)
- Peaches and strawberries as garnish

### Directions

- Add the peaches, strawberries, sugar, as well as 1 cup of water in a small saucepan. Bring to a simmer, then reduce to low heat and continue to cook until the sugar has melted. Cook for another 5 to 10 min on low to mellow the peaches. Allow cooling after removing from the heat. Remove the fruit and keep the syrup refrigerated.
- Make your tea by boiling eight cups of water and soaking the tea bags in it. Cool the tea in a pitcher in the refrigerator.
- Once ready to serve, add the strawberry & peach syrup to the tea. Either the pitcher, as well as individual portions, were sweetened. Tea should be served with fresh strawberries & peaches.

## 6. FROZEN COCONUT MOJITO

Serving: 4

Preparation time: 30 min

Nutritional values: Calories-141kcal|Carbs-31g|Protein-0g|Fat-1g

### Ingredients

- 1/2 cup of sugar or stevia (baking)
- Mint leaves, 1/2 cup
- White rum, 6 oz.
- 2 cups of coconut milk (light) from a can
- 2 limes, juiced

### Directions

- Mint simple syrup: Combine sugar / baking stevia, one cup of water, and mint leaves in a medium saucepan. Bring to a simmer, then lower the heat and simmer for 10 minutes. Remove the mint leaves and set aside the simple syrup. Let it chill in a bottle for several hours or unless ready to serve. Alternatively, put it in the refrigerator for 10-15 minutes to become cold. However, don't let it get too cold.

- In a high-powered processor, combine the rum, coconut milk, juice of a lime, leftover mint simple syrup, and then ice while ready to serve.

- In four cocktail glasses, distribute the frozen mojito. If preferred, sprinkle with leaves of mint and roasted coconut flakes. Serve right away.

## 7. WATERMELON BASIL COOLER

Serving: 4

Preparation time: 10 min

Nutritional values: Calories-141kcal|Carbs-31g|Protein-0g|Fat-1g

### Ingredients

- One watermelon
- 5 to 6 basil leaves, fresh
- 3 to 4 Mint Leaves (Fresh)
- Lime juice (half a lime)

### Directions

- Discard any seeds from the watermelon before chopping it. Chop the basil as well as mint leaves & mix them in a blender.

- Taste and, if desired, add additional herbs.

- Serve chilled over ice cubes. Refrigerate for 1-2 days in a small airtight container. It's healthy to consume it right away.

## 8. CUCUMBER VODKA SODA

Serving: 4

Preparation time: 1 hr.

Nutritional values: Calories-99kcal|Carbs-0g|Protein-0g|Fat-0g

### Ingredients

- 1 1/2 cups of fresh cucumber juice; two to three seedless cucumbers
- 1/2 cup of lime juice, freshly extracted
- Half-cup of vodka
- ¼ cup of simple syrup
- 1–2 cups fizzy water, lemon is delicious

### Directions

- If you don't have a blender, mix peeled seedless cucumbers (approximately 2 of them) in a processor with some water. Using a fine-mesh sieve, pour the puree into a medium measuring cup.

- Mix the cucumber and lime juice, vodka, & simple syrup in a large pitcher. Chill for approximately 1 hour after thoroughly stirring. Pour one cup of cold seltzer water into the glass before serving. Taste and add additional simple syrup & seltzer if preferred. Top with lime slices & cucumber slices and serve over crushed ice.

## 9. SUMMER BERRY SANGRIA

Serving: 6

Preparation time: 1 hr.

Nutritional values: Calories-150kcal|Carbs-19g|Protein-0g|Fat-0g

### Ingredients

- 1 6 ounces. bottle rinsed fresh raspberries and blackberries
- 1 6 ounces fresh blueberry bottle, rinsed
- 1 container (16 ounces) fresh strawberries, sliced
- 1 bottle of Moscato Middle Sister
- 1/3 cup of liqueur (raspberry/strawberry)

## Directions

- Mix the berries, raspberry (as well as strawberry), liqueur, agave (if using), & Moscato wine in a mixing glass. Refrigerate for 1 - 3 hours.

- Add ice as well as seltzer to flavor before serving.

- As the sangria remains in the fridge, it becomes better. If you don't really want the berries to be mushy, refrigerate the Moscato, liqueur, & seltzer individually before mixing them all together with the berries just before presenting.

## 10. COCONUT MATCHA HORCHATA : MATCHATA

Serving: 6

Preparation time: 10 min

Nutritional values: Calories-270kcal|Carbs-60g|Protein-6g|Fat-3g

## Ingredients

Day one

- 1 1/4 cup of raw whole almonds
- 6 tbsp. white long-grain rice

Day two

- 2 tbsp. matcha (latte grade)
- 1/4 tsp. pure vanilla extract
- 2 tbsp. coconut cream, canned

## Directions

Day one

- Bring a large saucepan of water to a boil over the moderate flame if using whole raw almonds. Sauté the almonds for one minute in boiling water, then strain and rinse under cold water. Remove the almonds from their skins and throw away the skins.

- Dismantle the rice with the cinnamon in a high-powered food processor or blender until powdery.

- In a heat-proof plate, combine the roasted almonds & rice powder, then add 3 cups of hot water over the surface.

- Opt for an eight-hour or overnight soaking.

Day two

- Make the syrup by boiling the sugar in a small container with 1/4 cup ice water over moderate flame until the sugar is fully dissolved. Remove the pan from the

heat and put it aside.

- Place the soaking liquid into a blender, along with the simple syrup, 2 cups of ice water, matcha, extract of vanilla, coconut cream, as well as salt, and puree until creamy.

- Filter the solution through a fine mesh, nut sack, or cheesecloth strainer over a medium bowl, squeezing the fluid out of the pulp. Remove the pulp and throw it away.

- Serve cold horchata with ice. The horchata will preserve in the fridge for a few days (give it a good stir before serving if it's been lying for a while).

## 11. ORANGE PEACH MANGO SPRITZER

Serving: 14

Preparation time: 10 min

Nutritional values: Calories-120kcal|Carbs-19g|Protein-1g|Fat-0g

## Ingredients

- 84 oz. orange mango peach juice 1 1/2 crates - or your favorite flavor
- 1 white wine bottle
- 2 liters seltzer water bottle
- Garnish with orange slices

## Directions

- To stiffen one carton of juice, put it in the freezer.
- Put iced juice in a medium serving jar once ready to serve.
- In a large mixing bowl, combine the wine, the rest of the juice, as well as seltzer water. To mix, stir everything together.
- Garnish with orange slices on the side.

## 12. ROSE, LEMON, STRAWBERRY INFUSED WATER

Serving: 4

Preparation time: 5 min

Nutritional values: Calories-5kcal|Carbs-1g|Protein-0g|Fat-0g

### Ingredients

- Strawberries, a handful
- Pesticide-free rose petals from a bunch of roses
- 1 lemon, peeled and cut into pieces
- Water that has been filtered

### Directions

- Cover a jug halfway with all of the components and chill for a minimum of a couple of hours, ideally overnight.
- It may be served directly from the pitcher or strained into glasses. To transfer into the cups and gather the petals of flowers and fruit bits, use a tiny sieve as well as a ladle.
- That's all. Have fun.

## 13. SKINNY CHAMPAGNE MARGARITAS

Serving: 2

Preparation time: 10 min

Nutritional values: Calories-178kcal|Carbs-16g|Protein-0g|Fat-0g

### Ingredients

- 4 oz. lime juice, freshly squeezed
- 3 oz. silver agave tequila
- 2 tsp. agave syrup
- Champagne, 4 oz.
- Slices of lime, for serving

### Directions

- Load a cocktail shaker completely with ice and mix vigorously. Combine the lime juice (fresh), tequila, as well as agave syrup in a cocktail shaker. To ensure thorough mixing, give it a good shake.
- Fill 2 cocktail glasses halfway with the drink.
- Garnish with champagne & wedges of lime.
- Cheers.

## 14. WATERMELON & CUCUMBER MOJITOS

Serving: 8

Preparation time: 20 min

Nutritional values: Calories-160kcal|Carbs-24g|Protein-2g|Fat-1g

### Ingredients

- 1/2 mashed seedless watermelon
- 1/2 cup of pureed English cucumber
- 2 limes, freshly squeezed

- 1/2 cup of muddled mint
- 8 oz. iced vodka

### Directions

- Mash the watermelon & cucumber together in a processor or juicer. If using a mixer, strain the juice through a mesh sieve to remove the pulp and keep the liquid apart.

- Lime juice and mint should be muddled together with a slotted spatula or a muddler whether you have them. Shake the ingredients for 15-20 seconds in a mixer with ice. Strain the liquid into a wide pitcher.

- In a wide pitcher, combine the juice, vodka, as well as sparkling water.

- Pour into ice-filled glasses and enjoy.

## 15. FROSTED LEMONADE

Serving: 1

Preparation time: 5 min

Nutritional values: Calories-330kcal|Carbs-65g|Protein-6g|Fat-6g

### Ingredients

- 1 cup of lemon juice, freshly extracted
- Half cup of sugar
- 2 1/2 cup of water
- 2 cups of ice cream (vanilla)

### Directions

- In a container, combine the lemon juice as well as sugar and whisk until the sugar is completely dissolved.

- Stir in the water until it is well combined.

- Chill for a minimum of one hour before serving.

- In a blender, mix 1 cup of lemonade & ice cream, then blend until creamy and frothy.

- Divide into 2 glasses and serve with a lemon slice as a topping.

## 16. ORANGE AND SPICE HOT CHOCOLATE

Serving: 2-3

Preparation time: 10 min

Nutritional values: Calories-160kcal|Carbs-31g|Protein-3g|Fat-4g

### Ingredients

- 3 cups of non-dairy milk, sugar-free
- 1 cup of orange juice (100 percent pure)
- 1/4 cup of cocoa powder, sugar-free
- 1/4 cup of raw sugar, natural maple syrup, or sugar made from coconut nectar
- 1/2 tsp. ginger powder

### Directions

- Heat the milk & orange juice in a medium saucepan. Stir in the cocoa powder, sugar, cinnamon, ground ginger, and a sprinkle of salt until the cocoa powder is fully dissolved. Reduce to a low heat setting to keep the cocoa hot while ready to serve.

- Pour in individual glasses with any desired garnish.

## 17. LEMON GINGER DETOX TEA

Serving: 1-2

Preparation time: 10 min

Nutritional values: Calories-12kcal|Carbs-2g|Protein-0g|Fat-0g

### Ingredients

- 2 c. water

- 1 inch trimmed and finely diced ginger
- 1/4 tsp. turmeric, (optional)
- 1/4 tsp. maple syrup or raw coconut / natural sugar (optional)
- Juice of 1 large lemon

### Directions

- Peel away the skin of the ginger with a vegetable peeler & finely slice with a serrated knife.
- Add the water, diced ginger, juice of lemon, turmeric, as well as cayenne to a small saucepan or kettle and stir well. Warm over low to moderate heat unless steam rises from the kettle or the alarm blows.
- Wait for five min of cooling time before pouring into individual glasses with a little sugar and serve.

## 18. CARROT, PINEAPPLE & GINGER JUICE

Serving: 2

Preparation time: 10 min

Nutritional values: Calories-169kcal|Carbs-39g|Protein-3g|Fat-1g

### Ingredients

- 7–9 medium carrots
- 1/4 pineapple, flesh only (approximately 1 cup)
- 1-inch ginger knob scraped

### Directions

- Prepare the carrots by thoroughly scrubbing and rinsing them. You may keep the toppers on if they're in good condition. If not, cut around 1/2 inches from the top. You may juice the entire carrot if it has the leafy green tips, but the color of the juice may alter.
- Enjoy the juice, made as per the equipment.

## 19. BEST VEGAN CHOCOLATE MILKSHAKE

Serving: 2

Preparation time: 5 min

Nutritional values: Calories-197kcal|Carbs-45g|Protein-3g|Fat-2g

### Ingredients

- 2 cups of non-dairy ice cream (vanilla) or 3 chilled, diced bananas
- 1 cup of almond milk (unsweetened) (or coconut, soy, etc.)
- 2 tbsp. cacao (or cocoa powder)
- 1 tsp. vanilla extract
- Optional: 1 seeded date (or 1 tablespoon natural maple syrup)

### Directions

- Place all ingredients in a blender and mix until smooth.
- End up serving in frosty glasses with desired toppings, or enjoy simple.

## 20. VEGAN STRAWBERRY MILKSHAKE

Serving: 1

Preparation time: 5 min

Nutritional values: Calories-254kcal|Carbs-54g|Protein-3g|Fat-3g

### Ingredients

- 1 cup of strawberries, chilled
- 1 scraped and diced frozen banana
- 1 cup of almond milk (unsweetened) (plain/vanilla)

- 1 tbsp. natural maple syrup or 1 Medjool date, seeded
- 1 tsp. vanilla extract

## Directions

- In a blending cup, add all of the ingredients, then blend until creamy. Divide into separate glasses and garnish as desired.

# 21. MIXED BERRY YOGURT SMOOTHIE

Serving: 2

Preparation time: 5 min

Nutritional values: Calories-240kcal|Carbs-36g|Protein-5g|Fat-10g

## Ingredients

- 1 1/2 cup of berries (strawberries, raspberry, blueberry, and/or cherries) chilled
- Optional: 1 tiny banana (adds additional creaminess!)
- 1 cup of non-dairy yogurt, sugar-free (plain or vanilla)
- 1/2 cup of almond milk, sugar-free (plain or vanilla)
- Optional: 1 tsp. vanilla essence or crushed vanilla bean powder

## Directions

- Place all of the ingredients in a mixer and mix until smooth, pausing to wipe down the sides as required. As desired, add a dash of dairy-free milk or water.
- Serve with a straw or spoon in a glass. Alternatively, make a smoothie bowl by combining all of the ingredients in a bowl.

# 22. CHOCOLATE ALMOND BUTTER SMOOTHIE / SMOOTHIE BOWL

Serving: 2

Preparation time: 5 min

Nutritional values: Calories-334kcal|Carbs-37g|Protein-9g|Fat-19g

## Ingredients

- 2 medium bananas, refrigerated (pref. over-ripe)
- 1/4 cup of almond butter (or any favorite nut butter)
- Cocoa powder (2 tbsp.)
- 1 cup of almond milk (unsweetened)
- 3–4 cubes of ice

## Directions

- In a blender, combine the bananas, almond butter, chocolate powder, additional vanilla, milk, as well as ice cubes. Blend until creamy.
- End up serving in mid-sized dishes with your preferred toppings. Pour in a bowl with a couple of additional toppings for a more conventional smoothie. Use a slotted spoon or a broad straw.

# 23. CHOCOLATE CHERRY SMOOTHIE

Serving: 2

Preparation time: 5 min

Nutritional values: Calories-251kcal|Carbs-63g|Protein-5g|Fat-4g

## Ingredients

- 2 cups of cherries (frozen)

- 1 cup of almond milk (unsweetened) (plain/vanilla)
- 2 tbsp. cacao powder (organic)
- 1 tsp. raw maple syrup (optional) or 1 tiny Medjool date (pitted & diced)
- 2 tbsp. almond butter or 1 dollop protein powder (simple or vanilla)

### Directions

- Blend the ingredients in a blender until creamy, adding more milk as required.
- Serve with desired toppings as well as a spoon or even a straw to eat or drink. Enjoy it frequently.

## 24. BANANA SPLIT SMOOTHIE

Serving: 1

Preparation time: 5 min

Nutritional values: Calories-287kcal|Carbs-50g|Protein-21g|Fat-2g

### Ingredients

- One banana (chilled or fresh)
- 4 to 5 strawberries (natural) (frozen or fresh)
- Pineapple (1/3 cup) (chilled or fresh)
- 1 tbsp. chocolate powder
- 1 tsp. extract of vanilla

### Directions

- Combine all of the ingredients, excluding the cherries, until creamy (if using absolutely fresh fruits, you might also want to add 1/2 cup cubes of ice to the milk or water, and to use it in replacement of part of the liquids).
- Strain into a drinking glass and garnish with desired toppings before serving.

## 25. MANGO PINEAPPLE SMOOTHIE

Serving: 1

Preparation time: 5 min

Nutritional values: Calories-287kcal|Carbs-73g|Protein-3g|Fat-1g

### Ingredients

- 1 mango, chopped into pieces (approximately 1–1 1/2 cup) (fresh or frozen)
- 1 banana, chilled and cut into pieces
- Pineapple chunks (1 cup) (fresh or frozen)
- 1/2 – 1 cup almond milk or water
- Chia seeds, to be used as a garnish

### Directions

- In a blending cup, combine the mango, diced banana, chunks of pineapple, & water/milk and mix until creamy.
- Serve in a single cup with chia seeds on top.

## 26. FRESH GREEN HEMP SMOOTHIE

Serving: 1

Preparation time: 5 min

Nutritional values: Calories-283kcal|Carbs-45g|Protein-9g|Fat-10g

### Ingredients

- 1 banana, ripe
- 1 large or 2 tiny mandarins (or 1/2–3/4 cup fresh berries)
- A bunch of spinach
- 3 tablespoons hemp protein powder or 2 tbsp. hemp hearts (coated hemp seeds)

- 1/2 cup of filtered water + more water as required

## Directions

- In a blending cup, combine the sliced banana (ripe), mandarins, a bunch of spinach, hemp protein, filtered water, as well as ice cubes and mix until smooth, approximately 1 minute.

## 27. BLUEBERRY BANANA SMOOTHIE

Serving: 1

Preparation time: 5 min

Nutritional values: Calories-244kcal|Carbs-51g|Protein-4g|Fat-3g

### Ingredients

- 1 banana, chilled
- 1 cup of blueberries, chilled
- Nut butter (1 tbsp.) (peanut butter, cashew butter, almond butter)
- Cinnamon (1/4–1/2 tsp.)
- 1 cup of almond milk (unsweetened) (basic flavor or vanilla)

### Directions

- In a blender, combine all ingredients and mix until desired consistency is achieved, adding additional milk or water as required.

## 28. FRUITY CHIA SEED SMOOTHIE

Serving: 1

Preparation time: 5 min

Nutritional values: Calories-328kcal|Carbs-58g|Protein-7g|Fat-10g

### Ingredients

- 1 cup of fruit (frozen) (berries, mango, cherry and pineapple, etc.)
- 1 banana, ripe and fresh
- 1/2–3/4 cup of non-dairy milk or coconut water
- Chia seeds (2 tbsp.)

### Directions

- In a blender cup, combine the chilled fruits, banana, fluids, as well as chia seeds; cover and mix until smooth. As required, add additional liquids.

## 29. HOT PINK BEET SMOOTHIE WITH CITRUS

Serving: 1

Preparation time: 5 min

Nutritional values: Calories-219kcal|Carbs-34g|Protein-9g|Fat-1g

### Ingredients

- 1 tangerine or clementine, scraped and cut into pieces
- 1 scraped and sliced tiny beet
- 1/2 banana, ripe but not overripe, preferably chilled
- Chia seeds, 1 tbsp.
- 1 cup of almond milk (unsweetened)

### Directions

- Mix the clementine pieces, beet, berries (strawberries, raspberries etc.), banana, almond butter, 1 tbsp. Chia seeds, 1 cup of almond milk, extract of vanilla, as well as sea salt in an inverted blender. Blend until the mixture is totally smooth.
- Enjoy right away.

## 30. CHOCOLATE BANANA OAT BREAKFAST SMOOTHIE

Serving: 1

Preparation time: 5 min

Nutritional values: Calories-262kcal|Carbs-50g|Protein-8g|Fat-7g

### Ingredients

- 1 cup of non-dairy milk
- 1/4 cup of rolled oats
- 2 tbsp. almond butter (or nut/seed butter of choice)
- 1/2 tbsp. cocoa powder, sugar-free
- 1 banana, ripe but not overripe, preferably chilled

### Directions

- Incorporate non-dairy milk, rolled oats, butter (almond), cocoa powder, seeds (flax), extract of vanilla, ripe banana, salt, cinnamon (optional), protein powder & ice in an inverted blender (if using). Remove the cover and increase the blending speed to maximum. Pulse the smoothie until it is perfectly smooth and foamy. Enjoy right away.

## 31. BERRY BEET VELVET SMOOTHIE

Serving: 1

Preparation time: 5 min

Nutritional values: Calories-351kcal|Carbs-43g|Protein-11g|Fat-17g

### Ingredients

- 1 heaping cup of red berries, mixed
- 1 scraped and sliced tiny beet
- 1/2 banana, ripe but not overripe, preferably chilled
- 1 Medjool date, pitted
- 1 tbsp. cacao powder (pure)

### Directions

- Incorporate the berries, diced beet, ripe banana, date, cacao powder, butter (almond), juice of lemon, vanilla extract, and plant milk in an electric blender. Include any add-ons you're using as well. Pulse on maximum until the mixture is smooth & creamy. Serve into a glass &, if desired, top with shredded coconut butter as well as a sprinkling of cacao powder. Enjoy!

## 32. SPICED STRAWBERRY & GOJI BERRY SMOOTHIE

Serving: 1

Preparation time: 5 min

Nutritional values: Calories-197kcal|Carbs-30g|Protein-3g|Fat-5g

### Ingredients

- 1 cup of non-dairy milk
- 1 cup of strawberries (de-seeded)
- 1 banana, ripe, frozen if possible
- 1 tbsp. plump goji berries, steeped in water
- 1 tbsp. butter made from almonds

### Directions

- Blend the dairy-free milk, strawberries, ripe banana, goji berries, 1 tbsp. almond butter, any protein powder, cinnamon (optional), ginger, date (pitted), juice of lemon, as well as salt in an electric blender until smooth. Gradually increase the blender's speed to maximum. Blend until the mixture is totally smooth.

- Drink the spicy strawberry & goji berry smoothie right away.

## 33. DEEP TROPICAL VIBES GREEN SMOOTHIE

Serving: 1

Preparation time: 5 min

Nutritional values: Calories-207kcal|Carbs-33g|Protein-15g|Fat-2g

### Ingredients

- 1/2 cup freshly squeezed orange juice
- 1/2 cup of coconut water
- 1 tbsp. ginger juice (fresh)
- 2-3 kale stalks, diced
- 1 scraped, pitted, and diced Ataulfo mango

### Directions

- Incorporate the fresh orange juice, water (coconut), coconut milk yogurt, juice of ginger, salt, extract of vanilla, kale, diced mango, banana, as well as ice in an electric blender (if using). Pulse on maximum until smooth & creamy. Enjoy the deep green smoothie right away, topped with coconut flakes if desired.

## 34. VEGAN PEANUT BUTTER MOCHA SMOOTHIE

Serving: 1

Preparation time: 5 min

Nutritional values: Calories-240kcal|Carbs-36g|Protein-7g|Fat-7g

### Ingredients

- 1/2 cup of non-dairy milk, unsweetened
- 1 tsp. powdered cocoa
- Peanut butter (two tbsp.)
- 1 banana, ripe, chilled if possible
- 1 espresso shot

### Directions

- Incorporate the milk, preferred protein powder, rolled oats, powdered cocoa, peanut butter, extract of vanilla, salt, ripe banana, espresso, as well as ice in an electric blender. Increase the blender's speed to maximum, then continue to blend for approximately 30 seconds, or until the mixture is completely rich and creamy. Instantly drink the smoothie.

## 35. GINGER C & GREENS SMOOTHIE

Serving: 1

Preparation time: 5 min

Nutritional values: Calories-380kcal|Carbs-91g|Protein-6g|Fat-1g

### Ingredients

- 1 cup of orange juice
- Lemon juice, squeezed
- 2-inch piece of peeled and diced fresh ginger
- 1 scoop of protein powder, vanilla
- 2 cups of spinach (baby)

### Directions

- Incorporate the orange and lemon juice, chopped ginger, vanilla protein powder, cinnamon, extract of vanilla, salt, cayenne, spinach (baby), and refrigerated banana in an electric blender. Increase the blender's speed to maximum and continue to mix until the liquid is totally smooth. Enjoy right away.

## 36. VEGAN PUMPKIN SMOOTHIE WITH GINGER & CARDAMOM

Serving: 1

Preparation time: 5 min

Nutritional values: Calories-350kcal|Carbs-56g|Protein-2g|Fat-1g

### Ingredients

- 1/3 cup of pureed pumpkin
- 1/3 cup of coconut milk yogurt, simple
- 1/4 tsp. cinnamon powder
- 1/4 tsp. cardamom powder
- 1/2 tsp. fresh ginger, chopped

### Directions

- Incorporate pumpkin puree, yogurt, milk (almond), lemon juice, syrup (maple), ripe banana, ground cinnamon, ground cardamom, chopped ginger, extract of vanilla, as well as sea salt in an electric blender. Pulse the pumpkin smoothie on maximum until it is totally smooth & creamy. If desired, top the smoothie with a sprinkling of cinnamon, nut butter splatters, and more coconut yogurt

## 37. BEET & BLOOD ORANGE SPICE SMOOTHIE

Serving: 1

Preparation time: 5 min

Nutritional values: Calories-144kcal|Carbs-33g|Protein-3g|Fat-0g

### Ingredients

- 1 large scraped and sliced beet
- 1 blood orange, scraped and sliced into segments
- 1/2 banana, ripe but not overripe, preferably chilled
- 1 tbsp. butter made from almonds
- 1/4 tsp. cardamom powder

### Directions

- Incorporate the non-dairy milk, chopped beet, blood orange, banana, butter (almond), cinnamon, 1/4 tsp. cardamom, nutmeg, salt, juice of lemon, as well as ice in an electric blender (if using). Increase the blender's speed to maximum and pulse until the mixture is totally smooth. Immediately drink the beet & blood orange smoothie.

## 38. GOLDEN PEACH SUNRISE SMOOTHIE

Serving: 1

Preparation time: 10 min

Nutritional values: Calories-100kcal|Carbs-23g|Protein-2g|Fat-0g

### Ingredients

- 1/4 cup of raspberries, frozen or fresh, thawed
- 1 tiny orange, scraped and cut into wedges
- 1 large scraped and diced carrot
- 1-2 ripe chilled peaches (approximately 1 1/2 heaping cups of chilled peach pieces)
- 1-inch piece of peeled and diced ginger

### Directions

- Mush the berries with a spatula in a mixing bowl unless the juices begin to flow. This juice will be layered in between portions of the drink in the glass. You may filter off the seeds or left them if the consistency isn't an issue. Reserved the raspberry juice/purée.

- Mix the orange, chopped carrot, chilled peach, diced ginger, turmeric, powder (camu, camu) (if using), extract of vanilla, salt, pepper, juice of lemon, & water in an electric blender. Pulse on maximum until the mixture is creamy, rich, and smooth. If your blender comes with a tamper, now is the time to put it to good use!

- Fill a glass halfway with the smoothie. Drizzle a quarter of the raspberry puree on top after that. Continue with the rest raspberry juice & smoothie. Enjoy right away.

## 39. KIWI FRUIT SMOOTHIE

Serving: 2-3

Preparation time: 5 min

Nutritional values: Calories-163kcal|Carbs-36g|Protein-2g|Fat-1g

### Ingredients

- 3 kiwi fruits, peeled
- 1 peeled, bruised, and diced mango
- Pineapple juice
- 1 diced banana

### Directions

- Blend all of the contents in a blender until smooth, then divide into two large

glasses.

## 40. CREAMY MANGO & COCONUT SMOOTHIE

Serving: 2

Preparation time: 5 min

Nutritional values: Calories-212kcal|Carbs-22g|Protein-4g|Fat-11g

### Ingredients

- Coconut milk in a tall glass, half-filled
- 4 tablespoons of yogurt made with coconut milk
- One banana
- 1 tablespoon powdered flaxseed, sunflower, as well as pumpkin seeds
- 120g mango cubes, frozen

### Directions

- For speed, weigh all the contents or pour them into a large glass - things don't have to be precise. Place all of the ingredients in a blender and mix until smooth. Pour into one tall glass or two tiny tumblers.

- If using, slice the passion fruit in halves, then scatter the seeds on top.

# CHAPTER 4: VEGAN LUNCH RECIPES

## 1. GRILLED CAULIFLOWER WEDGES

Serving: 8

Preparation time: 30 min

Nutritional values: Calories-57kcal|Carbs-5g|Protein-4g|Fat-2g

### Ingredients

- 1 large cauliflower head
- 1 tsp. turmeric powder
- 1/2 tsp. red pepper flakes, crumbled
- 2 tbsp. extra virgin olive oil
- Lemon juice, excess olive oil, as well as pomegranate seeds are optional.

### Directions

- Remove the leaves off the cauliflower and trim the stem. Cauliflower should be cut into eight pieces. Combine the turmeric as well as pepper flakes in a bowl. Brush the wedges with oil and then top with the turmeric mixture.
- Grill, tented, over moderate flame for 8 to 10 min on all sides, then broil 4 inches from the flame once cauliflower is soft. Splash with the juice of a lemon and more oil, if preferred, then top with seeds of a pomegranate.

## 2. SPICY EDAMAME

Serving: 6

Preparation time: 20 min

Nutritional values: Calories-52kcal|Carbs-5g|Protein-4g|Fat-2g

### Ingredients

- 1 (16-oz.) packet of chilled edamame pods
- 2 tsp. salt (kosher)
- 3/4 tsp. ginger powder
- 1/2 tsp. of garlic powder
- 1/4 tsp. red pepper flakes, crumbled

### Directions

- Fill a wide saucepan halfway with water and add the edamame. Bring the water to a boil. Cook, covered, for 4-5 min or until translucent; drain. Place in a large mixing bowl. Stir in the spices to coat.

## 3. GARBANZO-STUFFED MINI PEPPERS

Serving: 32

Preparation time: 20 min

Nutritional values: Calories-15kcal|Carbs-3g|Protein-1g|Fat-0g

### Ingredients

- 1 tsp. seeds of cumin
- 1 can (15 oz.) washed & drained garbanzo beans/chickpeas
- 1/4 cup of cilantro leaves, fresh
- 16 tiny sweet peppers, sliced lengthwise
- 3 tbsp. cider vinegar

### Directions

- Sauté cumin seeds in a small clear pan over moderate heat until fragrant, about 1-2 minutes, tossing constantly. Place the mixture in a stick blender. Pulse the garbanzo beans, diced cilantro, water, vinegar, & salt until well combined.
- Spoon the mixture into the pepper halves. Add more cilantro on top if desired. Refrigerate until ready to serve.
- It can be consumed as an appetizer or lunch

## 4. WAFFLE-IRON ACORN SQUASH

Serving: 4

Preparation time: 15 min

Nutritional values: Calories-98kcal|Carbs-25g|Protein-1g|Fat-0g

### Ingredients

- Maple syrup (three tbsp.)
- 1 tiny acorn squash
- 3/4 tsp. powdered chipotle pepper
- 1/2 tsp. salt

### Directions

- Heat up a waffle maker that has been oiled. Combine the syrup, powdered chipotle pepper, & salt in a mixing bowl.
- Squash should be cut crosswise with 1/2-inch thick pieces. Cut out the centers of the squash using circular cookie cutters to remove the strands & seeds. If required, cut pieces in half to fit in the waffle maker.
- Bake for 3-4 min in a waffle machine, till soft and gently browned. Serve with the syrup mixture on top.

## 5. MINTY PEAS & ONIONS

Serving: 8

Preparation time: 20 min

Nutritional values: Calories-134kcal|Carbs-19g|Protein-6g|Fat-4g

### Ingredients

- 2 large onions, peeled and sliced into 1/2-inch wedges
- 1/2 cup of sweet red pepper, diced
- 2 tbsp. oil (vegetable)
- 2 packets (16 oz. each) peas that have been frozen
- 2 tbsp. fresh mint chopped
- 2 tsp. dried mint

### Directions

- Fry onions as well as red pepper in a wide pan in oil until onions tender slightly.
- Cook, uncovered, for ten min or until peas are cooked completely, stirring occasionally. Sauté for 1 minute after adding the mint.

## 6. CHILI-LIME ROASTED CHICKPEAS

Serving: 2

Preparation time: 50 min

Nutritional values: Calories-178kcal|Carbs-23g|Protein-8g|Fat-6g

### Ingredients

- 2 cans (15 oz. each) washed, drained, & pat dry chickpeas/garbanzo beans
- Chilli powder (1 tbsp.)
- 2 tsp. cumin powder
- 1 tsp. lime zest, shredded
- Lime juice, 1 tbsp.

### Directions

- Preheat the oven to 400 degrees Fahrenheit. Cover a baking sheet that is 15x10x1 inches. Remove any loose skins from the chickpeas and spread them out in a thin layer on foil. Bake for 40 to 45 min, tossing every fifteen minutes, until very crispy.
- Meanwhile, combine the other ingredients in a mixing bowl. Take out the chickpeas from the oven and set them aside for 5 minutes to cool. Sprinkle the oil mixture over the pan and shake it

## 7. CABBAGE & RUTABAGA SLAW

Serving: 2

Preparation time: 50 min

Nutritional values: Calories-126kcal|Carbs-19g|Protein-2g|Fat-6g

### Ingredients

- 2 cups of peeled and sliced rutabaga
- 2 cups of cabbage, finely diced
- 1/2 cup of red onion, coarsely diced
- 1/4 cup of fresh Italian parsley, diced
- 1/2 cup of apple cider vinaigrette (low-fat)

### Directions

- Toss all of the components together. Refrigerate for 3 hours, covered, to let ingredients combine.

## 8. HOMEMADE POTATO CHIPS

Serving: 8

Preparation time: 35 min

Nutritional values: Calories-176kcal|Carbs-24g|Protein-3g|Fat-8g

### Ingredients

- 7 medium potatoes, skinned and peeled (approximately 2 lbs.)
- Icy water (two quarts)
- Garlic powder, 2 tsp.
- 1 1/2 tsp. celery salt
- 1 1/2 tsp. pepper

### Directions

- Chop potatoes into thin slices using a potato peeler or a metal cheese cutter. Add the iced water & salt to a large mixing bowl. Soak for thirty min.

- Drain the potatoes and wipe them dry with paper towels. Mix the powdered garlic, celery salt, as well as pepper together in a medium bowl and put aside.

- Preheat 1-1/2 inch oil to 375° in a cast-iron as well as another hefty skillet. 3-4 minutes, turning frequently, sauté potatoes in portions until lightly browned.

- Put on paper towels using a slotted spoon. Sprinkle spice mixture over the top right away. Place the container in a sealed jar to keep it fresh.

## 9. CRUNCHY BREADSTICKS

Serving: 16

Preparation time: 40 min

Nutritional values: Calories-78kcal|Carbs-12g|Protein-2g|Fat-2g

### Ingredients

- 2 cups of flour (all-purpose)
- 1 1/2 tsp. baking powder
- Shortening, 3 tbsp.
- 1 tbsp. extra virgin olive oil
- 1/2 - 3/4 cup of cold water

### Directions

- Incorporate the flour, powder (baking), salt, plus shortening in a stick

blender; cover as well as a process until the batter resembles rough crumbles. Slowly add water whilst processing unless dough becomes a ball.

- Place on a floured surface to finish. Make a 10x8-inch rectangle out of the dough. Cut the 10x1/2-in. strands into sixteen pieces. Put each strand on a baking sheet after twisting it four times. Rub with oil. Toss the breadsticks with a mixture of coarse salt as well as thyme.

- Preheat the oven to 350°F and bake for 18-20 minutes, or until lightly browned and crisp. Allow cooling on a cooling rack.

## 10. WARM TASTY GREENS WITH GARLIC

Serving: 4

Preparation time: 30 min

Nutritional values: Calories-137kcal|Carbs-14g|Protein-4g|Fat-9g

### Ingredients

- 1 lb. pruned & torn kale (about 20 cups)
- 2 tbsp. extra virgin olive oil
- 1/4 cup of diced oil-packed sunflower seeds
- 5 chopped garlic cloves
- 2 tbsp. fresh parsley, chopped

### Directions

- Bring 1 inch of water to a simmer in a 6-quart stockpot. Cook, cover, and for 10 to 15 min or until kale is soft. Using a slotted spoon, remove the chicken and discard the cooking liquid.

- Add the oil in the same saucepan over medium heat. Cook and stir for 1 minute after adding the tomatoes & garlic. Cook, turning periodically, until the kale, parsley, and salt are tender.

## 11. SWEET POTATO KIEV

Serving: 4

Preparation time: 1 hr.

Nutritional values: Calories-323kcal|Carbs-41g|Protein-10g|Fat-10g

### Ingredients

- 4 tiny sweet potatoes (approximately 200g each), washed
- 1 Alpine bread piece
- 2 teaspoons lemon rind, chopped finely
- 3 chopped garlic cloves
- 1 large diced red onion
- 400g rinsed and drained can of cannellini beans
- 120 gram of baby spinach

### Directions

- Preheat the oven to 200 degrees Celsius/180 degrees Celsius fan-forced. Using the baking paper, line a baking pan. Pinch the potatoes (sweet) all over with a fork. Put on the tray that has been prepared. Cook for 50 minutes, rotating once, or until a skewer inserted into the center comes out clean.

- In a stick blender, blitz the bread until fine crumbles develop. Toss in the minced parsley, lemon rind, one-third of the garlic, and 1 tablespoon oil in a mixing bowl. Place aside.

- Meantime, in a wide non-stick frying pan, heat the remaining oil over low flame. Cook, occasionally stirring, for 6 to 8 min, or until the onion is cooked and lightly golden. Add the rest garlic & thyme. Cook, constantly stirring, for one minute or until fragrant. Cook for 2 minutes, stirring occasionally. Stir in the spinach until it is slightly wilted. Remove from the flame and season with salt and pepper.

- Snip a slit on the top of each cooked potato. With a fork, gently smash the flesh, then pour the mixture of onion into the slits. Place on a baking sheet. Put the breadcrumb mixture on top. Preheat oven to 350°F and bake for ten min, or until lightly browned. To serve, top with additional parsley leaves.

## 12. QUINOA, EDAMAME AND BROCCOLI SALAD

Serving: 1

Preparation time: 15 min

Nutritional values: Calories-304kcal|Carbs-24g|Protein-15g|Fat-14g

### Ingredients

- 75g of broccoli florets, chopped into tiny pieces
- 50g chilled edamame pods
- Cooked quinoa, 75g (1/2 cup)
- 75g of halved cherry tomatoes
- 2 teaspoon freshly squeezed lemon juice
- 1 tablespoon hummus

### Directions

- Steam, simmer or heat broccoli as well as edamame for two min, or until soft.

Drain. Under cool running water, rehydrate. Drain.

- In a serving dish, combine the broccoli, edamame, quinoa, as well as tomato. Add parsley as well as almonds to finish. Drizzle the lemon juice & oil over the top. Season. To dish out, top with hummus.

## 13. VEGAN TOMATO TART

Serving: 4

Preparation time: 2 hr.

Nutritional values: Calories-310kcal|Carbs-35g|Protein-7g|Fat-13g

### Ingredients

- 1 cup of raw cashews (145g)
- Tomato medley mix (800g)
- 1 tablespoon freshly squeezed lemon juice
- 1 tablespoon balsamic vinegar
- 8 fresh thyme sprigs, medium
- 1 thawed sheet of chilled low-fat vegan puff pastry

### Directions

- In a bowl, put cashews. Fill with water and set aside. Let soak for the night.

- Set the oven at 150 degrees Celsius/130 degrees Celsius fan-forced. Using the baking paper, prepare a wide baking tray. Arrange the tomatoes on the tray. Spritz with oil. Bake until tender, about 1 1/2 hours. To eliminate extra juice, gently press.

- Drain the cashews in the meanwhile. Pulse the basil in a blender. Pulse until the mixture is finely chopped. Combine the cashews, lemon juice, & 1/3 cup of water in a mixing bowl. Pulse for 2 to 3 min, scraping down the side of the jar as needed, or until creamy & smooth. Add the nutritional yeast. Season. Blend until smooth.

- Raise the temperature of the oven by approximately 210°C/190°C fan-driven. Using a little spray of oil, lightly coat an oven-safe frying pan. Mix in the vinegar & maple syrup. Boil for 1 to 2 minutes over medium heat, or unless the liquid thickens & covers the pan's bottom. Remove the pan from the heat.

- Over the syrup mixture, sprinkle the thyme. Tomatoes should be arranged neatly over the top, with any juices remaining on the tray. Place the puff pastry on top, tucking in the sides if necessary. Preheat oven to 350°F and bake for 20 to 25 min, or until lightly browned. Leave for a quick cooling period of 2-3 minutes.

- On top of the pastry, put a plate. Invert with care. Add more basil if desired. Pour half of the pesto cream on top. If using, sprinkle with rocket.

# 14. STUFFED ROAST PUMPKIN

Serving: 6

Preparation time: 2 hr.

Nutritional values: Calories-328kcal|Carbs-31g|Protein-14g|Fat-13g

## Ingredients

- 1.8kg butternut pumpkin (whole)
- 3 finely chopped garlic cloves
- 2 tiny red capsicums, deseeded and sliced into 1cm strands
- 2 deseeded tiny yellow capsicums, sliced into 1cm-thick strands
- 400g rinsed and drained brown lentils
- 150 gram of baby spinach
- 2 tablespoons pine nuts
- 2 asparagus bunches, pruned

## Directions

- Preheat the oven to 190 degrees Fahrenheit/170 degrees Fahrenheit with the fan on. Using the baking paper, prepare a large baking tray. The pumpkin should be cut in half lengthwise. Scrape out the seeds with a spoon. Put the pumpkin on the prepared pan, cut-side up. Apply a light coat of oil. Season. Bake for 1 hour and 10 minutes, or until vegetables are soft. Cut one onion into slices. The leftover onion should be thinly sliced. Let pumpkin settle before scooping off the flesh from each half, keeping a 3cm thick shell. Save the flesh.

- Next, in a wide frying pan over a moderate flame, heat the oil. Cook, occasionally stirring, for three minutes or until onion is translucent. Combine the garlic as well as paprika in a mixing bowl. Cook for one minute, stirring constantly. Cook, frequently stirring, for ten min or unless capsicum is just cooked. Combine the vinegar plus maple syrup in a mixing bowl. Cook for 10 to 15 minutes, stirring periodically, or until caramelized.

- Toss in the lentils and the pumpkin you set aside with the onion mixture. Season. Stir. Leave to cool slightly before serving.

- In a pot of boiling water, cook the spinach. Drain. Under cool running water, rinse. Squeeze off any extra liquid before chopping roughly. Pine nuts should be stirred into the lentil mixture.

- Divide the lentil mixture evenly among the pumpkin shells. Carefully assemble the pieces and clip at 2cm intervals with kitchen string. Replace the pumpkin in the tray. Toss in the onion slices. Cook for twenty minutes, or until asparagus is just soft, stirring halfway through. For five min, set aside. Remove the string. Using a knife, cut six thick slices. Place asparagus, onion, as well as a rocket on serving dishes. Drizzle over the balsamic vinegar.

# 15. QUINOA PILAF

Serving: 4

Preparation time: 40 min

Nutritional values: Calories-355kcal|Carbs-43g|Protein-13g|Fat-11g

## Ingredients

- 200g (1 cup) rinsed as well as drained quinoa
- Massel Salt Lowered Vegetable Broth Cubes (2 cups)
- 1 bunch of broccolini, sliced into 3cm segments and a half if stems are too long
- 1 large corncob (without kernels)
- 1 asparagus bunch, clipped and sliced lengthwise
- 2 tablespoons unsalted pistachio kernels, diced
- Pomegranate arils, 2 tablespoons

## Directions

- In a medium skillet, add the oil over high

temperatures. Cook for five min, or until the onion is translucent, stirring periodically. Cook, constantly stirring, for 1 min or until garlic is fragrant.

• Toss in the quinoa & stock. Bring the water to a boil. Reduce the heat to a low setting. Cover and cook for 12 minutes or until most of the stock has been absorbed. Combine the broccolini, corn, sliced asparagus, as well as peas in a large mixing bowl. To mix, stir everything together. Cook for two min, or until all of the stock has been absorbed. Remove the pan from the heat. Cast aside for 3 to 4 min to steam, covered.

• Season with salt and pepper after mixing in the spinach. Scatter the pistachios as well as pomegranate arils over the pilaf. Garnish with lime slices on the side.

## 16. MUSHROOM CACCIATORE PASTA

Serving: 4

Preparation time: 20 min

Nutritional values: Calories-554kcal|Carbs-67g|Protein-34g|Fat-16g

### Ingredients

• 375g pasta spirals (high-protein, low-carb) or any preferred pasta

• 500g thickly sliced tiny portobello mushrooms

• 1 deseeded red capsicum, roughly chopped

• Vegan pasta sauce (tomato) 500g bottle

• Massel Vegetable Liquid Broth, (1/3 cup)

### Directions

• Boil the spiral pasta until al dente according to the package instructions in a large pot of boiling water. Drain.

• In a wide, deep frying pan, warm half the oil over moderate flame. Sauté, often swirling, for approximately 3 minutes, or until the mushroom starts to soften. Pour the rest of the oil into the middle of the pan, pushing the mushrooms to the side. Combine the capsicum as well as parsley stems in a bowl. Cook for two minutes before mixing in the mushroom. Combine the pasta sauce (tomato), broth, lentils, and olives in a mixing bowl. Bring to a low boil, then reduce to low heat.

• Serve the pasta in separate serving dishes. Toss in the parsley leaves until they are evenly distributed throughout the mushroom concoction. Dish out the pasta with mushroom cacciatore on top.

## 17. CREAMY PUMPKIN, SAGE & BROCCOLI SPELT PASTA BAKES

Serving: 4

Preparation time: 55 min

Nutritional values: Calories-384kcal|Carbs-52g|Protein-16g|Fat-9g

### Ingredients

• 750g peeled and seeded butternut pumpkin

• 3 chopped garlic cloves

• 8 fresh leaves of sage + 1 tablespoon diced sage, plus

• 200g spelt spiral pasta, dry

• 300 g broccoli florets, chopped into tiny pieces

• Soy milk (1/2 cup)

### Directions

• Preheat the oven at 200 degrees Celsius/180 degrees Celsius fan-forced. Using the baking paper, prepare a baking pan. Put the pumpkin, onion, garlic, as well as sage on the tray that has been prepared. Sprinkle oil over the tray, then cover with foil. Preheat oven to 400°F and bake for 40 minutes, or until veggies are soft. Allow cooling slightly before serving.

- Meantime, prepare the pasta according to package instructions in a large pot of moderately salted boiling water, including the broccoli, in the final 3 minutes of cooking. Drain.

- Blend or pulse the pumpkin concoction in a stick blender until creamy. Combine the soy milk, yeast, & onion powder in a mixing bowl. Season after processing until thoroughly mixed.

- Reduce the temperature of the oven to 180°C/160°C fan-forced. Using a little spray of oil, lightly coat four 375ml (1 1/2 cups) oven-safe dishes. Combine the pumpkin and pasta in a mixing bowl. Toss everything together. Divide the mixture among the prepared plates. In a small dish, combine breadcrumbs and more sage. Breadcrumb mixture should be sprinkled over the pasta bakes. Bake for 15 minutes, or unless the breadcrumbs have become brown. Season to taste and serve.

## 18. CREAMY VEGAN SUN-DRIED TOMATO & BROCCOLINI GNOCCHI

Serving: 4

Preparation time: 10 min

Nutritional values: Calories-375kcal|Carbs-59g|Protein-10g|Fat-8g

### Ingredients

- 1 broccolini bunch
- 500g mini / standard size gnocchi in a 500g package
- Frozen peas, 150g (1 cup)
- 1 tablespoon oil from the jar, 100g of sun-dried tomato segments
- 1 tablespoon all-purpose flour
- 1 1/2 cups, So Delicious Almond Milk (Original)

### Directions

- Heat the kettle.

- Mash the garlic & snip the broccolini stems in half lengthwise, whereas the kettle is heating up. Over moderate flame, heat a wide frying pan.

- In a medium skillet over high temperature, add the boiling water. (If you fill it too high, this will take too much time to re-boil.) Boil until the gnocchi reaches the top, then add the peas & broccolini in the final minute of boiling. Drain.

- Pour in the saved sun-dried tomato oil once the skillet is heated. Cook, constantly stirring, for thirty seconds after adding the garlic. Toss in the flour. Cook for thirty seconds, stirring constantly. Take off from the heat and stir in the almond milk unless well mixed. Transfer the mixture to a moderate flame and simmer, stirring continuously, until it boils. Cook for 3 minutes, or till sauce gradually thickens. Season.

- Toss in the gnocchi concoction & tomato strips until everything is well combined. Season to taste, then divide into serving dishes and garnish with basil.

## 19. PASTA NOURISH BOWL

Serving: 4

Preparation time: 15 min

Nutritional values: Calories-318kcal|Carbs-28g|Protein-18g|Fat-13g

### Ingredients

- Spiral pasta, wholemeal, 125g
- 150 g snipped snow peas
- 1 tablespoon vinegar (apple cider)
- Tahini (1 tablespoon)
- 1 tablespoon lemon juice, freshly squeezed
- 200g tofu, diced (Japanese marinated)

### Directions

- Cook the pasta according to the package directions in a large pot of boiling water, incorporating the sugar snaps as well as snow peas just before cooking. Using cold running water, drain & refresh. In a large mixing bowl, combine all of the ingredients.

- Next, in a mixing bowl, whisk together the vinegar, maple syrup, and a generous sprinkle of salt. Toss in the cabbage to coat it with the dressing. Allow 10 minutes for the pickling to take effect. Drain.

- In a small mixing bowl, whisk together the tahini, lemon juice, oil, and 1 to 2 tablespoons warm water until translucent.

- Arrange pasta, pickled cabbage, carrots, as well as tofu in serving dishes. Splash the vinaigrette over the pepitas, then serve.

## 20. SWEETPOTATO NOODLES WITH CRISPY KALE

Serving: 4

Preparation time: 30 min

Nutritional values: Calories-779kcal|Carbs-80g|Protein-5g|Fat-39g

### Ingredients

- 1 kale bunch
- 2 tablespoons pine nuts
- 2 chopped large garlic cloves
- 1 lemon, coarsely grated rind
- 700g of sweet potato, scraped and spiralized into noodles

### Directions

- Heat the oven at 150 degrees Celsius/130 degrees Celsius fan-forced. Remove the stems from the kale and tear them into bite-size chunks. Put two large baking pans on top of each other. Use olive oil as a spray. Preheat oven to 350°F and bake for 10 to 12 minutes, or until crunchy. Leave to cool.

- Meantime, lay the pine nuts out on a baking sheet and bake for 3-5 minutes, until brown. Leave to cool

- In a wide, deep frying pan, mix the oil, garlic, chili, as well as lemon rind. Sauté for 3 minutes over a moderate flame, or unless the garlic begins to crackle. Raise the temperature to medium-high and incorporate the sweet potato noodles. Cook for five min, stirring the noodles halfway through, or unless the noodles are soft. Throw in half of the kale to mix.

- In serving dishes, distribute the noodle mixture. Distribute the leftover kale, as well as the pine nuts, over the top. Sprinkle with a bit more olive oil if desired.

## 21. CILANTRO POTATOES

Serving: 8

Preparation time: 45 min

Nutritional values: Calories-160kcal|Carbs-23g|Protein-2g|Fat-7g

### Ingredients

- 1 bunch of diced cilantro
- 1 chopped garlic clove
- 1/4 cup of extra virgin olive oil
- 3 lb. peeled and chopped potatoes
- 1/2 tsp. of salt

### Directions

- Cook cilantro as well as chopped garlic in oil for one minute in a wide cast-iron or any other heavy pan over moderate flame. Cook, occasionally stirring, until the potatoes are soft and gently browned, about 20-25 minutes.

- Drain. Season with salt.

## 22. LEMON GARLIC MUSHROOMS

Serving: 4

Preparation time: 15 min

Nutritional values: Calories-94kcal|Carbs-6g|Protein-3g|Fat-7g

### Ingredients

- 1/4 cup of lemon juice
- 3 tbsp. fresh parsley, chopped
- 2 tbsp. extra virgin olive oil
- 3 chopped garlic cloves
- 1 lb. fresh mushrooms, medium

### Directions

- To make the dressing, combine the first five ingredients in a mixing bowl. Toss the mushrooms with 2 tbsp. of the dressing and toss well.
- Cover and cook mushrooms over moderate flame until cooked, approximately 5-7 minutes on each side. While serving, toss with the residual dressing.

## 23. ROASTED ASPARAGUS & LEEKS

Serving: 12

Preparation time: 35 min

Nutritional values: Calories-83kcal|Carbs-15g|Protein-3g|Fat-2g

### Ingredients

- 3 lb. asparagus spears, clipped
- 12 large leeks, split lengthwise (white part only)
- 4 1/2 tsp. extra virgin olive oil
- Dill weed, 1 1/2 tsp.
- 1/2 tsp. red pepper flakes, crumbled

### Directions

- Put asparagus & leeks in a 15x10x1-inch baking pan that hasn't been oiled. Combine the other ingredients in a mixing bowl and pour over the veggies.
- Preheat oven to 400°F and bake for 20 to 25 minutes, or until vegetables are soft, turning periodically.

## 24. SPICY GRILLED EGGPLANT

Serving: 12

Preparation time: 35 min

Nutritional values: Calories-88kcal|Carbs-7g|Protein-1g|Fat-7g

### Ingredients

- 2 tiny eggplant halves, 1/2-inch thick
- 1/4 cup extra virgin olive oil
- Lime juice (two tbsp.)
- 3 tsp. Cajun seasoning

### Directions

- Using a brush, coat the eggplant slices in oil. Splash lime juice over the top and season with Cajun spice. Allow for a 5-minute rest period.
- Cover and grill eggplant over a moderate flame or broil 4 inches from the flame until soft, about 4-5 minutes on each side.

## 25. SIMPLE GUACAMOLE

Serving: 1-2

Preparation time: 10 min

Nutritional values: Calories-53kcal|Carbs-3g|Protein-1g|Fat-5g

### Ingredients

- 2 medium avocados, ripe
- 1 tbsp. lemon juice

- 1/4 cup of salsa chunky
- 1/8 tsp. to 1/4 tsp. salt

## Directions

- Place avocados in a mixing bowl after peeling and chopping. Add a squeeze of lemon juice. Toss in the salsa and season with salt, then mash roughly with a fork. Chill until ready to serve.

## 26. THYME SEA SALT CRACKERS

Serving: 1-2

Preparation time: 10 min

Nutritional values: Calories-23kcal|Carbs-3g|Protein-0g|Fat-1g

## Ingredients

- 2-1/2 cups of flour (all-purpose)
- 1/2 cup of whole wheat flour, white
- 3/4 cup of water
- 1 to 2 tbsp. fresh thyme, chopped
- 3/4 tsp. salt (sea or kosher)

## Directions

- Preheat the oven to 375 degrees Fahrenheit. Whisk together the flour as well as salt in a large mixing bowl. Mix with a fork as you slowly add water, then 1/4 cup oil until the dough sticks together when compressed. Divide the dough into three equal halves.

- Roll each piece of dough to 1/8-inch thickness on a gently floured surface. Using a floured 1-1/2-inch round cookie cutter, cut out the cookies. Place 1 inch apart on baking pans that haven't been greased. Using a fork, pierce each cracker and gently brush with the remaining oil. Scatter thyme as well as sea salt over crackers.

- Bake for 9-11 minutes, or until gently browned on the bottoms.

## 27. THYME ZUCCHINI SAUTÉ

Serving: 4

Preparation time: 15 min

Nutritional values: Calories-53kcal|Carbs-5g|Protein-2g|Fat-4g

## Ingredients

- 1 lb. medium zucchini, sliced & quartered crosswise
- 1/4 cup of onion, chopped finely
- 1 squashed vegetable bouillon cube
- 2 tbsp. fresh parsley, chopped
- 1/4 tsp. dried thyme or 1 tsp. coarsely chopped thyme

## Directions

- Heat the oil in a wide skillet over moderate flame. Cook & stir for 4-5 minutes, or unless zucchini is crunchy, adding zucchini, onion, & bouillon as needed. Garnish with herbs.

## 28. FRESH FRUITBOWL

Serving: 16

Preparation time: 15 min

Nutritional values: Calories-56kcal|Carbs-14g|Protein-1g|Fat-0g

## Ingredients

- 8 cups chunks of fresh melon
- Corn syrup, 1–2 tbsp.
- 1 quart sliced fresh strawberries
- 2 cups of pineapple cubes (fresh)
- 2 segmented oranges

## Directions

• Mix melon chunks plus corn syrup in a large mixing bowl. Chill overnight, covered. Toss in the other fruits just before serving. If desired, top with mint leaves (fresh).

## 29. GARLIC-CHIVE BAKED FRIES

Serving: 4

Preparation time: 25 min

Nutritional values: Calories-200kcal|Carbs-39g|Protein-5g|Fat-4g

### Ingredients

• 4 potatoes, medium russet
• 1 tbsp. of extra virgin olive oil
• 4 tsp. chives, chopped
• Garlic powder, 1/2 tsp.
• Pepper (1/4 tsp.)

### Directions

• Preheat the oven to 450 degrees Fahrenheit. Slice potatoes into 1/4-inch julienne strips. Wash well & dry with a clean cloth.

• Fill a big mixing bowl halfway with potatoes. Spray with oil and add the rest of the ingredients. Toss to evenly distribute the ingredients. Coat two 15x10x1-inch baking trays with cooking spray and place them in a single layer.

• Cook for 20 to 25 minutes, rotating once or until gently browned.

## 30. ROASTED RADISHES

Serving: 6

Preparation time: 40 min

Nutritional values: Calories-88kcal|Carbs-6g|Protein-1g|Fat-7g

### Ingredients

• Radishes, cut & quartered, 2-1/4 lb. (approximately 6 cups)
• 3 tbsp. extra virgin olive oil
• 1 tsp. dried oregano or 1 tbsp. chopped fresh oregano
• Salt (1/4 tsp.)
• 1/4 tsp. of pepper

### Directions

• Preheat the oven to 425 degrees Fahrenheit. Toss the radishes with the rest of the ingredients. Place in a greased 15x10x1-inch baking pan.

• Roast for 30 minutes, tossing once, until crisp-tender

## 31. FAST FRUIT SALSA

Serving: 1-2

Preparation time: 10 min

Nutritional values: Calories-48kcal|Carbs-13g|Protein-0g|Fat-0g

### Ingredients

• 1 unsweetened chopped pineapple can (8 oz.), drained
• 1 mandarin orange can (8 oz.), drained & diced
• 1/4 cup of red onion, minced
• 1 tbsp. cilantro, chopped Tortilla chips

### Directions

• Mix the pineapple, diced oranges, chopped red onion, & cilantro in a large mixing bowl. Cover and chill until ready to serve. Toss with tortilla chips before serving.

## 32. GARLIC-ROSEMARY BRUSSELS SPROUTS

Serving: 8

Preparation time: 35 min

Nutritional values: Calories-134kcal|Carbs-15g|Protein-5g|Fat-7g

### Ingredients

- 4 chopped garlic cloves
- 1 tsp. kosher salt
- 2 lbs. (approximately 8 cups) clipped and sliced Brussels sprouts
- 1 cup of bread crumbs (panko)
- 1 to 2 tbsp. fresh rosemary, chopped

### Directions

- Preheat the oven to 425 degrees Fahrenheit. In a medium microwave-safe dish, combine the first four ingredients; heat on high for 30 seconds.
- Combine Brussels sprouts with 3 tbsp. oil mixture in a 15x10x1-in. skillet. Roast for ten minutes.
- Combine bread crumbs, chopped rosemary, and the remaining oil mixture in a mixing bowl; scatter over sprouts. Bake for 12 to 15 minutes, or until crumbs are golden brown & sprouts are soft. Serve right away.

## 33. JICAMA CITRUS SALAD

Serving: 10

Preparation time: 15 min

Nutritional values: Calories-76kcal|Carbs-19g|Protein-1g|Fat-0g

### Ingredients

- 8 trimmed, sliced, and chopped tangerines
- 2 shallots, finely sliced
- 1 lb. large jicama, peeled & diced
- 2 tbsp. lemon juice/lime juice
- 1/4 cup of fresh cilantro, minced

### Directions

- Put all ingredients and chill until ready to serve.

## 34. ROASTED BEET WEDGES

Serving: 4

Preparation time: 1 hr. 15 min

Nutritional values: Calories-92kcal|Carbs-12g|Protein-2g|Fat-5g

### Ingredients

- 1 lb. scraped large fresh beets
- 4 tsp. extra virgin olive oil
- Kosher salt (1/2 tsp.)
- 3–5 rosemary sprigs, fresh

### Directions

- Preheat the oven to 400 degrees Fahrenheit. Put each beet on a wide plate and cut it into six wedges. Toss gently with olive oil & salt to coat.
- In a 15x10x1-inch baking tray, place a 12-inch-long strip of heavy-duty foil. Arrange the beets on foil and sprinkle with rosemary. Wrap the foil around the beets and firmly seal them.
- Bake for 1 hour or until the potatoes are soft. Carefully open the foil to let steam escape. Remove rosemary sprigs and discard.

# 35. SWEETPOTATOES WITH KALE AND CARAMELIZED ONIONS

Serving: 6

Preparation time: 35 min

Nutritional values: Calories-157kcal|Carbs-22g|Protein-3g|Fat-7g

## Ingredients

- 3 medium sweet potatoes, peeled & cubed
- 1 bundle of kale stems, cut into bite-size chunks
- 1 finely sliced medium onion
- 2 tablespoons avocado oil or olive oil, separated
- 1 teaspoon of salt, divided

## Directions

- Preheat the oven at 375 degrees Fahrenheit. Use parchment paper/foil to prepare the baking sheet. Put sweet potatoes, 1 tablespoon oil, 1/2 teaspoon salt, & 1/4 teaspoon pepper. Toss everything together and bake for 25 to 30 minutes, or unless sweet potatoes are tender. Toss once halfway through. Remove and put aside.

- Preheat the pan over medium-low heat in the meanwhile. Cook, constantly stirring, until the remaining 1 tablespoon of oil, the onion, and 1/4 teaspoon of salt are soft. Reduce heat to low & simmer, stirring periodically, until onions begin to caramelize, approximately 25 minutes.

- Sauté for 5-10 minutes, until the kale leaves start to wilt & mellow, with the remaining 1/4 teaspoon salt and 1/4 teaspoon pepper in the pan.

- Stir in the cooked sweet potatoes to mix everything. Add more spices and a sprinkle of olive oil if desired.

# 36. BAKED GARLIC PEPPER POLENTA FRIES

Serving: 45

Preparation time: 50 min

Nutritional values: Calories-225kcal|Carbs-16g|Protein-4g|Fat-17g

## Ingredients

- 1 pre-made polenta tube (18 ounces)
- 2 tablespoons olive oil
- 1 teaspoon black pepper, freshly crushed
- 1 teaspoon powdered garlic
- 1/2 teaspoon salt

## Directions

- Preheat the oven to 450 degrees Fahrenheit.

- Cast aside a cookie sheet lined with parchment paper.

- Cut the polenta in half lengthwise. Each half should be cut in half lengthwise. Then, lengthwise, slice each quarter into thirds. Next, cut each third into 3 to 5 fries lengthwise.

- Arrange the fries on a parchment-lined baking sheet in a thin layer.

- Season with salt and pepper, then spray with olive oil.

- Remove the fries from the oven after 20 minutes and rotate them.

- Bake for another twenty minutes, or until desired crispiness is reached.

- Eat alone or with a dipping sauce.

- Enjoy.

## 37. ARRABBIATA BEANS

Serving: 4

Preparation time: 15 min

Nutritional values: Calories-355kcal|Carbs-59g|Protein-9g|Fat-7g

### Ingredients

- 6 garlic cloves, finely chopped
- 1 tsp. crushed red pepper
- 1 tomato sauce can (15 oz.)
- 1/2 cup of fresh parsley (or 1/4 cup dried parsley)
- 2 cans (15.5 oz. each) excellent northern beans

### Directions

- In a medium saucepan, heat the oil over moderate flame.
- Combine the garlic, flakes of red pepper, and a sprinkle of salt in a small mixing bowl. Cook, occasionally stirring, until the garlic begins to brown, about 2-3 minutes.
- Toss in ½ cup of water as well as tomato sauce. Reduce the heat to a low setting and stir occasionally.
- Leave the sauce to simmer for a minimum of ten minutes.
- Rinse the beans and combine them with the sauce while ready to serve. Leave the beans to simmer for a few minutes. Toss in the parsley with the sauce. Toss to mix and serve with a sprinkle of Parmesan cheese on top, if preferred. Sprinkle with salt, pepper, & Parmesan cheese to taste.

## 38. ROASTED CAULIFLOWER GARLIC HUMMUS

Serving: 4-6

Preparation time: 35 min

Nutritional values: Calories-156kcal|Carbs-5g|Protein-3g|Fat-14g

### Ingredients

- 1 natural cauliflower head, average to large
- Avocado oil (1/4 cup)
- Tahini (1/4 cup)
- Lemon juice, 1/3 tbsp.
- 4-6 garlic cloves

### Directions

- Preheat the oven to 425 degrees Fahrenheit.
- Cauliflower should be chopped and washed.
- Cook for 20 minutes with the cauliflower & garlic cloves, then turn & cook for a further fifteen min.
- Remove from the oven and set aside to cool for five min.
- In a food processor or blender, combine the remaining ingredients.
- Pulse until the mixture is completely smooth and creamy.
- If preferred, top with more lemon juice & avocado oil.

## 39. BESTDRY SAUTED MUSHROOMS

Serving: 4

Preparation time: 12 min

Nutritional values: Calories-35kcal|Carbs-2g|Protein-1g|Fat-2g

### Ingredients

- 1 lb. of mushrooms

- A pinch of salt
- 1/4 teaspoon freshly ground pepper
- 1 teaspoon oil (olive, sesame), ghee, or butter
- 1 teaspoon liquid aminos (soy sauce, coconut aminos, etc.)

## Directions

- Preheat a large cast-iron skillet over medium heat. Cook, stirring periodically, for 5 to 7 minutes after adding the mushrooms. There's no need to put anything at this stage since the mushrooms will emit their own juice.
- When the mushrooms are tender, season with salt, liquid aminos, & oil or ghee, and continue to simmer for further 2 minutes.
- If preferred, garnish with parsley and serve immediately.

# 40. CASHEW CREAM CHEESE

Serving: 5

Preparation time: 25 min

Nutritional values: Calories-28kcal|Carbs-1g|Protein-0g|Fat-3g

## Ingredients

- 1 cup of soaked uncooked cashews
- 1 tbsp. coconut oil (refined)
- 3-5 tbsp. lemon juice, freshly squeezed
- 1/2 tsp. pink Himalayan salt

## Directions

- In a food processor, combine the soaked cashews, coconut oil, lemon juice, & salt.
- To attain a creamy consistency, pulse for 5-8 minutes. During the mixing stage, stop the machine and wipe down the edges 2 to 3 times.
- Taste and adjust the seasoning with extra lemon juice and salt as required.
- Refrigerate for seven days if stored in an airtight container.

# 41. SEA SALT CHICKPEA CRACKERS

Serving: 5

Preparation time: 35 min

Nutritional values: Calories-48kcal|Carbs-1g|Protein-0g|Fat-5g

## Ingredients

- 1 cup of garbanzo bean flour (chickpeas)
- 1 tsp. powder of baking
- 1/2 tsp. sea salt / pink salt, plus a little more for sprinkling
- Water (three tbsp.)
- 2 tbsp. extra virgin olive oil

## Directions

- Preheat the oven to 350 degrees Fahrenheit.
- Add all ingredients to a wide mixing bowl.
- Mix the dough until it clumps together & can be molded into a ball.
- Place the ball of dough on a chopping board or worktop lined with parchment paper. Using flour, dust the surface. Turnover and dust with flour once more.
- Roll out to a thickness of approximately 1/8 inch.
- Cut the ball of dough into the appropriate shapes with a pizza cutter/knife.
- Using a moist fork, pierce the tops. Season with salt.
- Move the parchment paper to a baking sheet, dough and all.

- Bake for twenty minutes, or until everything is crisp, golden, and darkening at the edges.
- Leave it to cool fully before slicing and serving.
- Enjoy.

## 42. RED LENTIL FLAT BREAD PIZZA CRUST

Serving: 10

Preparation time: 6 hr. 30 min

Nutritional values: Calories-61kcal|Carbs-11g|Protein-5g|Fat-1g

### Ingredients

- 1 cup red lentils, soaked for 24 hours
- 1 cup of water
- 1 clove of garlic
- 1 teaspoon of salt
- Half teaspoon of baking powder
- Extra virgin olive oil

### Directions

- Soak the lentils with water in a closed jar or dish.
- Soak for at least six hours or overnight.
- Drain and rinse the lentils.
- Preheat the oven to 425 degrees Fahrenheit. Cast aside a cookie sheet lined with parchment paper.
- In a high-speed blender, combine soaked lentils and 1/2 cup water. Blend until completely smooth.
- Combine the garlic, salt, as well as baking powder in a mixing bowl. Blend well.
- Drizzle olive oil over the parchment-lined cookie sheet.
- Spoon the flatbread batter upon parchment paper and spread into the desired shape with the edge of a spatula, approximately 1/4-1/2 inch thick. Drizzle a little olive oil on top.
- Bake for 20 to 25 min, or until stiff and brown around the sides.
- To serve, top with preferred toppings* and enjoy as is, or broil for several minutes for pleasant toppings.
- Enjoy.

## 43. REFRIED BLACK BEANS

Serving: 8

Preparation time: 30 min

Nutritional values: Calories-196kcal|Carbs-15g|Protein-4g|Fat-8g

### Ingredients

- 1 lb. black beans (dried)
- 1/2 tsp. Jamaican Jerk BBQ Spices 3 Cups of Water
- 1/2 tsp. garlic powder
- 1/2 tsp. onion powder
- To taste, salt & pepper

### Directions

- In the Instant Pot, add black beans, water (3 cups), jerk spice, garlic & onion powder, as well as salt/pepper.
- Adjust the valve of pressure to closure and close the lid.
- Cook for 35 minutes on Manual Elevated Pressure (also known as pressure cooking). Let for a 25-minute organic release of pressure. Release any residual pressure manually.
- Blend until the appropriate consistency is achieved, adding additional water if required. If you want, you may also mix. Season with salt and pepper to taste.

# 44. BETTER THAN TRADER JOE'S CAULIFLOWER GNOCCHI

Serving: 4

Preparation time: 55 min

Nutritional values: Calories-181kcal|Carbs-42g|Protein-3g|Fat-0g

## Ingredients

- 1 1/2 cups mashed cauliflower (steamed)
- One & half-cup of cassava flour
- 1/3 cup of arrowroot powder; potato starch may be used.
- 1 teaspoon of salt
- Optional: 1/3 cup of rosemary, basil, or another herb of choice

## Directions

- Until the cauliflower is tender enough to puree, steam it. You can do it on the burner or in the microwave, with some water in a skillet and the cauliflower covered, although it cooks on moderate flame.
- Put the cauliflower (along with any optional herbs) in a stick blender and purée until smooth. There must be no clusters, and it should be creamy.
- Mix the cauliflower puree, flour of cassava, arrowroot powder, as well as sea salt in a large mixing bowl. Using a silicone spoon or a spatula, combine the ingredients until they form a dough. It must resemble bread dough in appearance.
- Bring a pan of water to a simmer while you set the bowl aside. Start making the gnocchi, whereas the water heats up.
- Distribute the dough into four equal pieces (they don't have to be exactly the same size), and dust a clean surface with cassava flour.
- Wrap a quarter of the dough into a large stick, then cut into 1" broad gnocchi. They don't need to be accurate.
- Rep with the whole dough, then put to a simmer in the pot.
- When the water boils, pour a little amount of olive oil (approximately 1 tsp.) to prevent the gnocchi from adhering together, and swirl the water vigorously to form a spiral. Carefully drop up to ten gnocchi into the whirling water and cook while they float to the surface. They're ready to be taken out at that point.
- Put the gnocchi on a clean dish after removing them from the water. Carry on with the rest of the gnocchi in the same manner.
- Eat it with your favourite sauce & protein.

# 45. ARROZ VERDE - MEXICAN GREEN RICE

Serving: 6

Preparation time: 35 min

Nutritional values: Calories-224kcal|Carbs-40g|Protein-5g|Fat-5g

## Ingredients

- 1/2 lb. spinach, fresh rinsed & clipped, tightly packed
- 1 pepper (poblano) Peeled, grilled, as well as seeded
- 1 cup of cilantro, chopped
- 2 green onions, coarsely chopped
- 2 cups of water
- 2 tablespoons oil (vegetable)
- 1 1/2 cups of white long-grain rice
- 1 teaspoon of salt

## Directions

- To eradicate all grit as well as sand from spinach, wash it well in a basin.

- Add and pulse the spinach, cilantro, chopped green onion, roasted poblano pepper, & one cup of water in a stick blender. (When finished, the puree should be approximately 2 cups.)

- In a non-stick skillet, heat the vegetable oil over medium flame. Add the rice, then toast it gently, often turning to avoid burning or sticking.

- Toss the rice with 2 cups of spinach mixture, 1 cup water, & salt. Stir the mixture to a simmer, then wrap with a tight-fitting cover, reduce to medium heat, and cook for 15 minutes.

- Take off from the heat and let aside for 10 minutes, completely covered.

- Serve the arroz verde with a spatula to fluff it up.

## 46. NON-CREAMY POTATO SALAD

Serving: 8

Preparation time: 30 min

Nutritional values: Calories-2209kcal|Carbs-264g|Protein-49g|Fat-114g

### Ingredients

- 10 to 12 medium potatoes
- 2 coarsely diced sweet onions (Spanish or Vidalia)
- 1/2 cup of vegetable or canola oil, split in half
- 1/4 cup of vinegar, white
- 2 tablespoons salt
- Black pepper, 2 teaspoons

### Directions

- Clean any dirt from the potatoes by washing them.
- Bring the potatoes to a simmer with their skins on. Drain the water as well as chill the potatoes until they are safe to handle.

- Finely cut the onions, then put them in 1/4 cup oil & 1 teaspoon salt for approximately 15 minutes.

- Scrape the peels off the potatoes after they have cooled. Cooked, scraped potatoes should be cut into tiny, bite-sized chunks.

- Mix the potatoes, onions, white vinegar, and the rest of the oil, salt, & pepper in a mixing bowl. Toss until everything is well mixed.

- If preferred, sprinkle with parsley before serving.

## 47. TIKKA MASALA WITH ROASTED VEGETABLES

Serving: 4

Preparation time: 40 min

Nutritional values: Calories-352kcal|Carbs-29g|Protein-5g|Fat-24g

### Ingredients

- 4 cup veggies, chopped into chunks of tougher vegetables, such as potatoes, beets, & winter squash, should be cut smaller, while peppers, onions, and summer squash should be sliced larger.
- Fresh herbs, whatever herbs you like, such as oregano, sage, as well as rosemary, would work well here.
- Coconut oil (about 1/3 cup)
- 1 tsp. kosher salt
- Black pepper, 1/8 teaspoon
- Maya Kaimal Tikka Masala Sauce (vegan), 1 jar

### Directions

- Start by chopping up your preferred veggies and putting them on the baking tray with your chosen herbs, salt, & pepper.

- Melt 1/3 cup of coconut oil & evenly pour it over the veggies.
- Cook for 30 to 35 min at 425°F, or until tender & slightly golden.
- In a non-stick frying pan, place the roasted vegetables.
- Add the whole bottle of Maya Kaimal Tikka Masala sauce (vegan) to the pan.
- Serve immediately after heating the veggies and sauce until they are hot.

## 48. CHICKPEA FAJITAS

Serving: 4

Preparation time: 25 min

Nutritional values: Calories-129kcal|Carbs-13g|Protein-3g|Fat-8g

### Ingredients

- 1 can of chickpeas (cooked) or dry chickpeas (cooked)
- 4 portobello mushrooms (or any other tiny mushrooms)
- 4 diced bell peppers
- 1 chopped red onion
- Fajita spices (3 tbsp.)
- 2 tablespoons extra virgin olive oil
- 1 tsp. kosher salt
- 1/4 tsp. black pepper, powdered

### Directions

- Prepare the vegetables first, then put them on a cookie sheet. Sprinkle with olive oil & season with fajita or taco spice, as desired.
- Mix everything together to evenly cover the chickpeas & vegetables with oil and spices.
- Roast for fifteen min at 180°C (356°F), turning halfway through. Check to see whether the chickpeas are crunchy enough unless they need to be roasted longer.
- Serve in bowls, over burned tortilla bread, or over rice.

## 49. CURRIED CAULIFLOWER SOUP

Serving: 4-6

Preparation time: 1 hr. 5 min

Nutritional values: Calories-131kcal|Carbs-14g|Protein-5g|Fat-7g

### Ingredients

- 2 lb. head of cauliflower
- 1 unsalted butter/ghee stick (4 oz.) Use coconut oil if you're a vegan.
- 1 leek, just the white & light green portions, divided lengthwise, thinly sliced, and thoroughly rinsed
- 2 tiny onions, divided and thinly sliced, half set aside for crispy onions
- 1 & 1/2 tbsp. of curry powder
- 1 tbsp. of cumin seeds, whole (optional)
- Salt & pepper
- 5 c. water

### Directions

- Remove the exterior leaves off the cauliflower, then trim the stalk. Trim around the core with a paring knife to remove it; thinly slice the core and set it aside. Cut one cup of half-inch lobes from the cauliflower head and put it aside. Cut the leftover cauliflower into half-inch-thick slices lengthwise.
- In a medium skillet, melt three tbsp. butter/ghee over moderate flame. Add the leek, chopped onion, powder of curry, as well as 1 1/2 tsp. salt; sim-

mer, often stirring, for approximately 7 minutes, or until the leek & onion are cooked but not charred.

- Raise the temperature to medium-high, then add the water, cut core, then 1/2 of the chopped cauliflower & bring to a simmer. Reduce the heat to moderate and cook for 15 minutes, stirring occasionally.

- Reduce to a low boil, add the remaining diced cauliflower, and cook until the cauliflower is soft, approximately 15-20 minutes.

- Then, in a wide frying pan, sauté the leftover chopped onion in three tablespoons, butter or ghee until light brown and crispy, turning periodically. Reserve.

- Cook leftover cauliflower florets in the same pan with 2 tablespoons butter, often turning, until light brown & butter is caramelized and aromatic, approximately 6-8 minutes. Season florets to perfection with salt and black pepper in a dish; keep leftover butter in the skillet for dripping.

- Toast entire cumin seeds for 1 to 2 minutes over a moderate flame, stirring pan constantly, until they bubble and sizzle.

- In a high-speed blender, puree the soup in batches. If the soup is too viscous, add more water.

- Reserve the florets and top each bowl with crispy onions as well as cumin seeds. Pour warmed browned butter into each bowl.

## 50. INSTANTPOT CILANTRO LIME BLACK BEANS

Serving: 8

Preparation time: 9 min

Nutritional values: Calories-77kcal|Carbs-24g|Protein-9g|Fat-4g

### Ingredients

- 2 cups dry black beans + 2 inches of water drench beans for 24 to 48 hours, drain, wash, and cook water must cover the wet beans by 2 inches in the Pot (instant)
- 1 1/2 tsp. salt (adjust to taste)
- 1 tsp. powdered garlic
- 1 tsp. of cumin
- 1/3 cup of coarsely diced fresh cilantro
- 2 limes juiced

### Directions

- Put the beans to the stainless steel base of the Instant Pot once they've been soaked, strained, and washed.

- Soak the beans with plenty of water to cover them by 2 inches.

- Examine the seal and close the vent before replacing the lid on the Pot.

- Set the timer to 9 minutes on maximum pressure by pressing the "Manual" / "Pressure Cook" switch. Let the pot gradually drop pressure for ten min after it beeps, then remove the remaining pressure.

- Combine the salt, powder of garlic, cumin, diced cilantro, & lime juice in a mixing bowl. If you want a stronger lime taste, add some zest of lime as well. To mix, stir everything together.

- Serve and have fun.

## 51. QUINOA FLATBREAD PIZZA CRUST

Serving: 1

Preparation time: 25 min

Nutritional values: Calories-119kcal|Carbs-17g|Protein-4g|Fat-4g

### Ingredients

- 3/4 cup of raw quinoa, soaking overnight
- 1/4 cup of water
- 1 clove of garlic

- 1 tsp. powder (baking)
- 1 teaspoon of salt
- Extra virgin olive oil

## Directions

- Weigh out the raw quinoa, put it in a container, fill it with water, and let it soak overnight before making this pizza.
- The quinoa must have subsumed the majority of the water by the following day. Cast aside the washed and drained quinoa.
- Set the oven at 425 degrees Fahrenheit. Cast aside a cookie sheet lined with parchment paper and drizzled with olive oil.
- Mix quinoa (raw), water, a clove of garlic, baking powder, and salt in a stick blender. Pulse until you get a creamy batter.
- Pour the batter onto the parchment paper that has been greased. Distribute and shape the batter with your hands or a spoon until it's approximately 1/2 inch thick.
- Take out from the oven after 15 minutes. Turn the crust gently over, and if necessary, onto a fresh piece of greased parchment paper.
- Transfer the pizza to the oven after topping it with the preferred ingredients*.
- Bake for another ten min, then broil for 2 to 4 minutes, or until the crust has reached the required brown bubbling crunchiness.
- Enjoy.

## 52. EASY PEA SOUP

Serving: 4

Preparation time: 15 min

Nutritional values: Calories-139kcal|Carbs-21g|Protein-6g|Fat-4g

## Ingredients

- 1 tbsp. of olive oil
- 1 diced onion
- 3 cups of vegetable broth
- 3 cups of peas, refrigerated

## Directions

- In a wide saucepan, add the oil, then put the onion & simmer for five min on low flame, until tender but not brown.
- Cook for another 5 minutes after adding the broth.
- Toss in the peas, return to low heat, and cook for an additional five min, or unless the peas are tender.
- In a mixer or with an electric blender, pulse the soup. Enjoy.

## 53. GLUTEN-FREE TORTILLAS

Serving: 16

Preparation time: 25 min

Nutritional values: Calories-104kcal|Carbs-17g|Protein-2g|Fat-3g

## Ingredients

- 2 c. water
- 2 cups of rice flour (brown)
- 2 tablespoon tapioca flour
- 2 tablespoons grape-seed or olive or avocado oil
- 1/2 teaspoon salt

## Directions

- Bring water to a simmer in a skillet over high temperatures. When the water has reached a boil, turn off the heat.
- In a large mixing bowl, add the rest of the ingredients and whisk vigorously until well mixed. Allow it to cool for approximately 7-8 minutes be-

fore stirring.

- Put the dough on a parchment-paper-lined chopping board or worktop and knead it until it forms a uniform round ball.

- Divide the dough into sixteen rounded tbsp. portions. Form the dough into neat balls.

- Over moderate flame, warm a non-stick or cast iron pan.

- Tapioca starch should be used to dust the parchment paper. Put 1 dough ball piece on top, then cover with another layer of parchment paper. Spread out the dough among parchment paper sheets with a rolling pin until you have 1 thin circular tortilla shape.

- Carefully peel aside the parchment paper from the tortilla and put it on the heated skillet.

- Cook for 1-2 minutes on one side, then turn and cook for another 1-2 minutes until both sides start to brown.

- Continue with the rest of the dough.

- Serve immediately, or put in a tea towel and refrigerate for up to four days, or freeze!

- Enjoy.

## 54. CHEESY OIL-FREE KALE CHIPS

Serving: 2

Preparation time: 1 hr.

Nutritional values: Calories-115kcal|Carbs-12g|Protein-7g|Fat-6g

## Ingredients

- 1 bundle of curly / lacinato kale
- 1 1/2 tablespoons tahini
- 1 tablespoon mustard (stone ground)
- Apple cider vinegar, 2 teaspoons
- 1 tablespoon of nutritional yeast
- Dash of salt

## Directions

- Preheat the oven at 250 degrees Fahrenheit (120 degrees Celsius) and prepare two large baking pans with parchment paper.

- Combine the 1 1/2 tbsp. tahini, 1 tbsp. mustard, 2 tsp. vinegar, 1 tbsp. nutritional yeast, as well as a sprinkle of salt in a medium mixing bowl. Using a fork, combine the ingredients. It will have a viscous, paste-like texture.

- Kale should be washed and dried. Trim the stems & cut the leaves into 3 × 3-inch segments. Shapes that aren't perfectly round are also acceptable. The kale dries more evenly when it is cut into tiny, similar-sized pieces. Bake time should be increased by 5-10 min.

- Rub the sauce (cheesy) into the greens with your fingertips. It's better to use a thin coat. Arrange the kale in a thin layer on the prepared pans. Overlapped pieces will not dry.

- Cook for 20 minutes, or unless the kale is crispy and dry. Serve immediately or allow to cool fully before storing.

## 55. PUMPKIN LENTIL SOUP WITH GINGER

Serving: 4

Preparation time: 20 min

Nutritional values: Calories-200kcal|Carbs-33g|Protein-10g|Fat-4g

## Ingredients

- 1 tbsp. extra virgin olive oil
- 1 trimmed and finely diced yellow onion
- 400 g of cubed pumpkin (approximately 4 cups), scraped and diced
- 400 g of cubed pumpkin (approximately 4 cups), scraped and diced

- 3/4 cup of red lentils 135g, rinsed & drained
- 4 cups of vegetable broth (1 litre/1 quart)
- 1 inch freshly grated fresh ginger

## Directions

- In a heavy-bottomed skillet or soup pan, heat the olive oil (extra virgin) over moderate flame. Cook for 3 minutes or until the onion is tender.
- While incorporating the finely shredded ginger, mix in the diced pumpkin, lentils, & broth.
- Cook for fifteen minutes over a low heat, or unless the pumpkin, as well as lentils, are tender.
- If necessary, season with a little salt.
- In a processor or with a stick blender, carefully mix the soup until smooth before serving.

## 56. INSTANT POT GARLIC RICE

Serving: 5

Preparation time: 15 min

Nutritional values: Calories-288kcal|Carbs-59g|Protein-5g|Fat-2g

## Ingredients

- 2 cups rice (basmati)
- 2 garlic heads (or twenty garlic cloves)
- 2 teaspoons extra virgin olive oil
- 1/4 tsp. turmeric powder
- A pinch of salt
- Mustard seeds (1 tsp.)
- 1/2 tsp. Urad dal

## Directions

- In the Instant Pot, select sauté & add 2 teaspoons of oil, mustard seeds, & urad dal. Cook them until their golden brown.
- Cook until the garlic is brown, then incorporate the minced garlic.
- Combine the washed rice, turmeric powder, salt, as well as 2 1/4 cup of water in a large mixing bowl. To halt the sautéing, click 'Cancel' and mix well.
- Lock the instant pot cover and adjust the timer for four minutes high pressure on the 'pressure cook' option.
- When the timer goes out, make a natural release.
- Remove the cover from the rice & ruffle it with a fork. Garlic rice from the Instant Pot is ready to eat.

## 57. CHICKPEA FLOUR PANCAKE -FENNEL & OLIVE

Serving: 2

Preparation time: 25 min

Nutritional values: Calories-232kcal|Carbs-26g|Protein-8g|Fat-11g

## Ingredients

- 1/2 cup of chickpea flour
- 1/2 cup of water
- 1/2 fennel bulb
- 1/4 cup pounded olives
- 1 garlic clove (or garlic salt)

To make the sauce

- 2 tablespoons vinegar
- 2 tablespoons of water
- Mustard (1 tablespoon)
- A teaspoon of maple syrup

## Directions

For filling

- Chop the fennel into pieces. Cut the olives into slices. Garlic cloves should be chopped or crushed (if using).

- Take a saucepan and put it on low heat. For 7 minutes, fry the fennel in a little extra virgin olive oil (or a tablespoon or two of water). After that, put the olives & garlic and continue to cook for a further five min.

For pancakes

- While it is going on, combine the chickpea flour & salt in a mixing bowl (or garlic salt). Add in the water whilst thoroughly stirring the mixture with a fork. Use the whisk if you have one.

- Preheat a skillet over medium heat, stir the olive oil, then pour half of the batter into it.

- Cook for about 4 to 5 min. Sauté for a further 4 to 5 minutes after turning. The pancake should be crispy when done.

For sauce

- Combine the vinegar, water (2 tbsp.), olive oil (extra virgin), mustard, maple syrup, salt, & pepper in a mixing bowl.

- Serve the pancakes when they're done. Spread the fennel-olive mixture on the plate and top with a sprig of fresh basil. Toss it all together with a generous dollop of mustard sauce.

## 58. SMOOCHING MUSHROOMS ON TOP

Serving: 1

Preparation time: 12 min

Nutritional values: Calories-329kcal|Carbs-57g|Protein-16g|Fat-7g

### Ingredients

- 7 med-sized mushrooms
- One apple (preferably green & sour)
- 1 garlic clove
- 1 bunch fresh parsley
- 2 wholegrain bread slices (or toast)
- 1 teaspoon extra virgin olive oil
- 1 teaspoon ground pepper
- 2 tablespoons soy sauce

### Directions

- In a medium-sized pan, add the oil.

- Finely diced the mushrooms & added them to the pan, stirring occasionally.

- Peel & slice the apple, then cut it into 4 pieces, consume two of them, and slice the remaining two into thin tiny pieces to incorporate into the mushrooms.

- Cook, constantly stirring, until the mushroom has softened.

- Add the garlic to the mixture by slicing, chopping, or smashing it.

- Stir for little or no more than 1 minute.

- Reduce the heat to low and whisk in the soy sauce.

- Make a toast in the meanwhile.

- Remove the pan from the heat and toss in the parsley & pepper.

- Enjoy the mushroom mixture on two pieces of bread.

## 59. POTATO STUFFED PEPPERS

Serving: 5

Preparation time: 25 min

Nutritional values: Calories-320kcal|Carbs-58g|Protein-8g|Fat-6g

### Ingredients

- 10 large red peppers (approximately 2 pounds)

- 1 pound potatoes
- 2 coarsely diced onions
- 4 tablespoons vegetable oil (olive or other)
- 1 teaspoon of black pepper
- Paprika, 2 teaspoon
- Optional: 1 teaspoon garlic powder
- 1 teaspoon savory (dry)

## Directions

- Trim the pepper tops & scrape the seeds. Peel and cut the potatoes as finely as possible.
- Put the olive oil in a skillet or saucepan and sauté the onion until transparent. Cook for 5 to 6 minutes, or until the potatoes are tender. It's okay if the potatoes begin to brown a little; just keep stirring to prevent burning.
- Combine paprika, powder of garlic, black pepper, salt, as well as any additional spices you're using in a mixing bowl. Take off from the heat after thoroughly mixing.
- Cover the peppers with the prepared potatoes, pushing them firmly to ensure no hollow areas remain.
- In a baking dish, distribute the peppers. If there are any potatoes left over that didn't fit inside the peppers, pour them across in the pan.
- Bake at 390°F/ 200°C for approximately 20 minutes, or unless the potatoes are fully cooked and the peppers begin to brown on the upper side.
- Serve right away.

## 60. SMOKED TOFU & HUMMUS BUDDHA BOWL

Serving: 2

Preparation time: 15 min

Nutritional values: Calories-399kcal|Carbs-51g|Protein-19g|Fat-13g

## Ingredients

- 1/2 teaspoon turmeric
- 1/2 cup rice (basmati)
- Smoked tofu, 10 oz.
- 2 teaspoons extra virgin olive oil
- 2 c. lettuce (lamb)
- 1 red onion, medium
- 4 tablespoons hummus
- 1 tablespoon of lemon juice
- 6 tablespoons of water
- 1/2 teaspoon salt

## Directions

- Cook the rice as per the package directions. Combine the turmeric & salt in a mixing bowl. Use chilled water, bring to a boil, then cover and let to boil for ten min.
- To prepare the smoked tofu, dice it. Then, in a medium-sized skillet, heat the extra virgin olive oil, then add the chopped tofu. Cook for around 7 minutes.
- Clean the lettuce (lamb) and chop the red onion thinly. Then, in the bowl, combine the two.
- Combine the hummus, juice of lemon, & water in a small bowl. Mix thoroughly.
- To assemble: in a mixing bowl, combine the cooked rice as well as fried tofu. Pour the hummus dipping over it at this point. If desired, sprinkle with salt.
- Enjoy.

## 61. VEGAN ZUCCHINI CORN FRITTERS

Serving: 4

Preparation time: 30 min

Nutritional values: Calories-205kcal|Carbs-35g|Protein-6g|Fat-6g

### Ingredients

- 1 cup all-purpose or whole grain flour
- 2 teaspoons of baking powder
- 1 flax/chia egg 1 tablespoon chia/ground flax seeds Plus 3 tbsp. water
- 1/2 cup of almond milk (or nut milk of choice)
- 1 1/2 cup shredded, squeezed, & drained zucchini
- 1 ear of corn kernels (cob removed)
- 1/2 coarsely chopped jalapeno pepper
- 3 garlic cloves, chopped
- 3 chopped scallions
- 1 tablespoon lime/lemon juice
- Serve with vegan sour cream and marinara sauce.

### Directions

- Shred two medium-sized zucchini (approximately 1 1/2 cup) into a dish or strainer lined with a hygienic dish towel/cheese cloth. Allow ten min after adding a pinch of salt. Using the towel's corners (as if it were a trash bag), bend the edge of the cloth across a sink or dish until the zucchini is squeezed and the extra liquid is drained. Squeeze out enough liquid as possible.
- In a small dish, combine three tbsp. of water and one tbsp. of chia seeds or powdered flax seeds. Wait five min for the mixture to settle.
- Combine the dry ingredients in a mixing bowl. Stir in the chia egg, milk (almond), & olive oil (extra virgin) with a whisk once more.
- Shred zucchini, corn kernels, coarsely diced jalapeno, chopped garlic, sliced scallions, as well as chopped parsley into a large mixing bowl. Lime juice should be sprinkled on top. Combine all of the ingredients.
- Preheat a skillet over medium heat and add one or two tbsp. of oil. Pour one heaping spoonful of batter each fritter and cook in batches for approximately 5 minutes each side over moderate flame. After turning, cover.
- Garnish the fritters with a salad or sauce of your choice

## 62. LENTIL BEAN SALAD

Serving: 2

Preparation time: 25 min

Nutritional values: Calories-362kcal|Carbs-64g|Protein-23g|Fat-2g

### Ingredients

- 3/4 cup dry red lentils
- 1 kidney bean can (drained & rinsed)
- 1 red bell pepper
- 3–4 green onions
- To taste, salt & pepper
- 2 garlic cloves
- 1/2 cup pureed tomatoes
- 2 wholegrain bread slices

### Directions

- Whether using dry red lentils, follow package directions (or just combine one part of red lentils with 1.5 parts of water and a pinch of salt in a saucepan). Bring to a simmer, then reduce to low heat and cook the lentils for 12 to 15 minutes, based on how tender you want them. Once the lentils are done, sprinkle with a touch of salt. Instead, for added flavor, boil them in vegetable broth).
- Meanwhile, chop the bell pepper as well as spring onions. Mince the garlic as well.
- Toss all of the components, such as the lentils & beans, into a large mixing bowl.
- Finally, if used, incorporate the tomato sau-

ce, mix it in, taste it, then season with salt & pepper one last time if required.

- Ready.

# 63. SPEEDY VEGAN BURRITO

Serving: 4

Preparation time: 20 min

Nutritional values: Calories-316kcal|Carbs-35g|Protein-11g|Fat-16g

## Ingredients

- Smoked tofu (7 oz.)
- One onion
- 1 green bell pepper
- 1 tablespoon extra-virgin olive oil
- 1 cup diced canned tomatoes (or four tablespoon tomato paste)
- One avocado
- Four wraps
- 1 teaspoon tabasco sauce (or sriracha, incorporated with the tomatoes)

## Directions

- To prepare the tofu, cut it into little squares. Chop the onion as well as bell pepper into small pieces.
- Heat the oil (olive) and cook the tofu, onion, as well as pepper for approximately 15 minutes on low flame.
- Remove the avocado's flesh using a spoon.
- Season the canned tomatoes with salt and black pepper. Add a dash of hot sauce if desired.
- Heat fresh tortilla wraps after the tofu mixture are done
- Distribute a tablespoon of tomato paste across each wrap if using. Place the tofu mixture in the centre of each wrap. Then, if using, create a line of canned tomato and a few avocados.
- Wrap the base up slightly initially, then wrap firmly around each side. Nothing would be able to get through to the other side.
- If desired, top with a dollop of soy yogurt.
- Finally, the vegan burritos are prepared.

# 64. VEGAN CHEESE SAVOURY SANDWICH FILLING

Serving: 4-6

Preparation time: 10 min

Nutritional values: Calories-237kcal|Carbs-10g|Protein-1g|Fat-20g

## Ingredients

- 120 g shredded vegan cheddar
- 1/2 red onion, coarsely diced 1 large carrot, shredded
- 6 tablespoons vegan mayonnaise
- 1 teaspoon mustard (American)
- 1 tsp. salt
- 1 tsp. black pepper

## Directions

- In a large mixing bowl, combine the veggies.
- Mix in the mayonnaise, mustard, salt, as well as pepper.
- Taste to check if additional salt or pepper is required.
- Enjoy.

# 65. RAUNCHY SWEET POTATO SALAD

Serving: 2

Preparation time: 30 min

Nutritional values: Calories-519kcal|Carbs-54g|Protein-8g|Fat-33g

## Ingredients

- 1 medium sweet potato (400g / 14oz)
- 1 avocado (ripe)
- Ten cherry tomatoes
- 2 tablespoons cashews
- 2 cups of salad (baby leaves)
- Lime, one (zest & juice)

## Directions

- Preheat oven at 180°C/360°F.
- Sweet potatoes should be cut into tiny pieces. Mix them in a dish with 1/2 tsp. salt as well as a drizzle of olive oil then set them on a baking sheet and bake for 25 minutes, or until tender.
- ½ of the avocado should be mashed, and the other half should be chopped into chunks. Chop the tomatoes (cherry) into halves. Put the zest of lime and juice, as well as the cashews, into a mixing bowl.
- Sprinkle with pepper & salt, as well as a drizzle of extra virgin olive oil.
- Allow the sweet potato to cool slightly before adding it to the bowl.
- Stir in the salad with a vigorous toss. Ready.

## 66. VEGETABLE HERB PASTA SALAD

Serving: 2

Preparation time: 25 min

Nutritional values: Calories-330kcal|Carbs-59g|Protein-11g|Fat-7g

## Ingredients

- 1 packet of gluten-free pasta (12 oz.)
- 1 English cucumber, large, unpeeled
- 2 large bell peppers, seeded & diced (any colour)
- 10 oz. (approximately 1 1/2 cup) cherry tomatoes halved
- 1/2 large coarsely chopped red onion

Vinaigrette with Lemon and Herbs

- 2 tablespoons lemon juice (approximately 2 lemons)
- 1 tablespoon of lemon zest
- 2 tablespoons of red wine vinegar
- 2 teaspoon of roughly chopped garlic
- 2 teaspoons of finely diced chives
- 2 teaspoons of coarsely chopped fresh dill

## Directions

- In a wide saucepan of salted water, cook the pasta. Cook as per package directions or until al dente.
- Make the salad dressing whilst pasta is cooking. In a medium mixing bowl, mix together all of the components until well mixed. Place aside.
- Strain the pasta in a colander, then rinse with cool water until no heat remains. In a wide mixing bowl, combine all of the ingredients.
- Toss the pasta salad with all of the veggies and the salad dressing. Mix all of the contents together until they are evenly covered. If needed, season with more salt and pepper. You may serve this right away or prepare it ahead of time.

## 67. CRISPY BUFFALO TOFU WRAP

Serving: 6

Preparation time: 50 min

Nutritional values: Calories-358kcal|Carbs-39g|Protein-15g|Fat-21g

## Ingredients

- 1 extra-firm 14-oz. tofu block, washed & pressed
- 1 cup of rolled oats, blended till coarse breadcrumbs
- Avocado oil (two tbsp.)
- Corn-starch (six tbsp.)
- 1/3 cup of oat milk, unsweetened
- 1 tbsp. coconut oil / vegan butter
- Buffalo sauce, 3/4 cup
- 6 wraps made with whole wheat
- Favourite toppings

## Directions

- Heat up the oven at 425 degrees F and put aside a wide baking sheet lined with parchment paper.
- Arrange 24 tiny rectangles of pounded tofu on a large dish or bowl and put them aside.
- Cast aside crushed oats, avocado oil, smoked paprika, oregano (dried), salt, & pepper in a wide shallow bowl. Pour oat milk into one of the shallow dishes and corn-starch to the other.
- Set up the assembly line for dipping. To start coating the tofu, dredge it with corn starch. After that, dab it in the milk (oat) and then let the excess drip out before tossing it in a mixture of bread crumbs. Put the covered tofu rectangles on the baking sheet that has been prepared. Continue with the entire tofu, allowing a minimum of 1 to 2 inches among each piece of coated tofu.
- Bake for thirty min after all of the tofu rectangles have been breaded.
- In a wide saucepan over moderate heat, melt the vegan butter/coconut oil whilst tofu is baking. Stir in the sauce (buffalo) after the butter/oil has melted. Lower the heat and cook the tofu until it is done.
- After the tofu has finished cooking, gently move the baked tofu chunks to a big mixing bowl or food storage jar. Spoon the buffalo sauce over the top & toss gently to mix. Make the wraps with tofu & your favourite toppings. Cover in foil or even a recyclable wrap and keep in the refrigerator for convenient lunches during the week.

# 68. TEMPEH SANDWICH

Serving: 2

Preparation time: 10 min

Nutritional values: Calories-547kcal|Carbs-51g|Protein-21g|Fat-32g

## Ingredients

- 4 wholemeal bread pieces
- Tempeh (3 oz.) (In 8 slices)
- Rocket, 2 handfuls (arugula)
- 1/2 cup oil-soaked sun-dried tomatoes
- 1 tablespoon extra-virgin olive oil
- 2 tablespoons vinegar (balsamic or wine vinegar)
- 2 tablespoons soy sauce
- 2 teaspoon maple syrup
- One avocado
- 1/2 lemons (juiced)
- To taste, salt & pepper

## Directions

- Sauté the tempeh in oil after slicing it. Mix the soy sauce, vinegar, as well as maple syrup after a few minutes. Simmer for a further 3 to 4 minutes, stirring occasionally.

- Slice the dried tomatoes in the meanwhile.
- Remove the avocado flesh and place it in a bowl with the lemon juice, salt, & pepper. Mix everything together.
- Half of the pieces of bread should be covered with avocado.
- Wash the rocket, then arrange it over the bread pieces. Toss in the dried tomatoes, diced.
- Place the tempeh on the rocket pieces of bread when it's done.
- On top of it, put the avocado bread. Done.

## 69. AUBERGINE CURRY - EGGPLANT CURRY

Serving: 2

Preparation time: 35 min

Nutritional values: Calories-459kcal|Carbs-65g|Protein-7g|Fat-18g

### Ingredients

- 1/2 cup rice (basmati)
- One aubergine (medium)
- 1 onion, red
- 2 garlic cloves
- 1 teaspoon curry powder or garam masala powder
- 1 teaspoon turmeric powder
- 1 teaspoon coriander powder
- 1 tin of chopped tomatoes (approximately 14oz/400g)
- 1 1/2 cup of coconut milk (low fat)

### Directions

- Cook the rice as per the package directions.
- Make tiny cubes out of the aubergine. Cook for 3-4 minutes at high temperature in a deep pan with olive oil. So that it doesn't heat up, make sure you stir it well.
- Meanwhile, chop the onion and toss it in as well. Return to moderate heat, then cook for another 5-6 minutes.
- Grind or chop the garlic.
- Add the garlic (chopped), garam masala, turmeric, as well as powdered coriander and stir to combine. Cook for 3 to 4 minutes more, stirring often.
- Combine the diced tomatoes & coconut milk in a mixing bowl. Season with salt. Cook for fifteen min at a low temperature. Stop cooking once the coconut milk has thickened to your preference. If you really like it a bit sweeter, add the sugar as well as mango chutney.
- Season to taste with salt & pepper.

## 70. PERUVIAN SANDWICH

Serving: 2

Preparation time: 20 min

Nutritional values: Calories-404kcal|Carbs-53g|Protein-11g|Fat-18g

### Ingredients

- 1 tbsp. of olive oil
- 2 tsp. powdered garlic
- 2 tsp. cumin powder
- 1 chopped zucchini (courgette)
- 1 deseeded red bell pepper, chopped into strips
- 5 washed & diced mushrooms

For pickled red onions

- 1 coarsely chopped red onion
- 1 lime's juice
- White vinegar, 2 tablespoons

## Directions

- Preheat the oven at 400 degrees Fahrenheit (200 degrees Celsius).

- In a large mixing bowl, combine the oil, seasonings, and salt and black pepper. Stir in the zucchini, pepper, then mushrooms to cover.

- Bake for fifteen minutes, or until the veggies are tender, in an even line on a baking sheet.

- Prepare the pickled onions in the meantime.

- Drain the finely diced red onion after rinsing it. Mix with the juice of lime and vinegar in a mixing bowl to cover. Allow for a ten-minute marinating period.

- Divide the rolls in half and add avocado pieces, pickled onions, roasted veggies, & parsley on top. Enjoy.

# CHAPTER 5: DELICIOUS VEGAN DINNER RECIPES

# 1. SEXY VEGAN LENTIL STEW

Serving: 2

Preparation time: 30 min

Nutritional values: Calories-420kcal|Carbs-73g|Protein-16g|Fat-7g

## Ingredients

- 1/2 cup of dry red lentils
- 1/2 cup of rice
- 2 garlic cloves
- 1/2 onion (medium)
- 1 tablespoon of tomato paste
- 1 cup of vegetable stock
- 2 c. water
- 1/2 teaspoon cumin
- 1 teaspoon turmeric powder
- 1 leaf of bay

## Directions

- Toast the cumin & cayenne pepper in a wide saucepan over low heat (no oil).
- Meanwhile, chop the onion & garlic.
- Stir the olive oil, garlic, as well as onion after the cumin starts to smell (typically after two or three minutes). Allow for 5 minutes of cooking time, stirring periodically.
- Toss in the tomato paste, red lentils, rice, vegetable stock, and water.
- Add the powder of turmeric, bay leaf, & thyme when it starts to boil. Cover and cook for 20-25 minutes on low heat. Every few minutes, give it a stir. To ensure the rice is done to your satisfaction, give it a quick taste test. Add the salt, stir thoroughly, and remove from the flame. Serve with paprika.

# 2. CHICKPEA FLOUR PANCAKES

Serving: 4

Preparation time: 10 min

Nutritional values: Calories-253kcal|Carbs-33g|Protein-10g|Fat-10g

## Ingredients

- 1 cup of besan/garbanzo flour (or chickpea flour)
- 1 cup of water
- 1 teaspoon turmeric powder
- 1/2 teaspoon salt
- 1/2 teaspoon pepper
- 3 onions (spring)
- 1 tablespoon extra-virgin olive oil

## Directions

- In a mixing bowl, combine the flour, water, 1 tsp. of turmeric, salt, pepper, as well as chili flakes (if using) and pulse or blend until smooth. Allow it to rest for several minutes whilst you prepare the oil/ghee in a non-stick skillet. The batter should be extremely runny!
- Finely slice the vegetables and toss them in with the other ingredients.
- To ensure that the base of the skillet is thoroughly covered with oil, use a napkin or something like (a spritz oil will work miracles here).
- While the pan is heated, add approximately a spoonful of the batter and the vegetables —moderate heat should suffice.
- Cook for approximately 3 minutes, or until the mixture begins to thicken up. You can create two pancakes simultaneously if you use two pans.
- If you want thin pancakes, make sure to use a wide skillet (or pans).
- Turn the pancakes with a wide spatula, ad-

ding additional oil below if required. The pancake would be done in around 2-3 min.

- Place it anywhere warm while you make the second pancake, using additional oil as needed.

- Done. Enjoy with your favourite toppings.

## 3. HIGH PROTEIN BLACK BEAN AND CORN SUMMER SALAD

Serving: 2

Preparation time: 10 min

Nutritional values: Calories-561kcal|Carbs-84g|Protein-18g|Fat-19g

### Ingredients

- 1 can of black beans (kidney beans are also good!) 15.5 oz. equals 1 can)
- 1/2 c. sweet corn (1 c. = 1.75 c. /15 oz.)
- 1 onion, red
- 2 onions (spring)
- 1/3 cup of couscous (instant)
- 1/2 cup stock (vegetable)
- 1 lemon (juiced)
- 2 teaspoon cumin
- 2 teaspoons chili flakes

### Directions

- Boil the water for the vegetable broth. Then, in a wide mixing bowl, ladle it over the couscous. Don't over-wet the couscous; the optimum water level is just enough to coat the grains. You may always add more if necessary; removing excess water is considerably more difficult.

- Cut the spring onions as well as red onions into half-slices.

- If you're using garlic, chop it up.

- The beans & corn should be drained and rinsed.

- The couscous must be done in about five min, then toss in the sliced onions, beans, & corn.

- Mix in the olive oil, juice of lemon, cumin, paprika powder, & chili flakes thoroughly.

- Eat it right away.

## 4. ARUGULA LENTIL SALAD

Serving: 2

Preparation time: 12 min

Nutritional values: Calories-529kcal|Carbs-73g|Protein-22g|Fat-19g

### Ingredients

- 1/2 cup of cashews (75 g = 1/2 cups)
- One onion
- 1 jalapeno / chilli
- 4 oil-soaked sun-dried tomatoes
- 3 pieces of bread (whole wheat)
- 1 cup of cooked brown lentils
- 1 arugula/rocket handful
- Balsamic vinegar, 2 tablespoons
- 1 handful of raisins
- 1 teaspoon of maple syrup

### Directions

- To maximize aroma, sauté the cashews in a skillet for approximately three minutes on low flame. After that, toss them on the salad plate.

- Slice the onion and cook it in olive oil (extra-virgin) for 3 min on low flame.

- Place the onion mixture in a large mixing bowl.

- Afterward, cut the dried tomatoes & chili/jalapeno. Make large croutons out of the bread.

Transfer them to the skillet & cook for an additional 2 minutes, or until the toast is crisp. The sun-dried tomato oil will suffice.

- Using salt and pepper, season to taste.
- Incorporate the arugula into the bowl after washing it. Toss in the raisins.
- Add the lentils as well. Add salt, pepper, maple syrup, & balsamic vinegar to taste. Finally, toss with the croutons mixture and serve.

## 5. VEGAN PEPPERONI PIZZA PANINI

Serving: 1

Preparation time: 15 min

Nutritional values: Calories-460kcal|Carbs-74g|Protein-28g|Fat-6g

### Ingredients

- 2 sourdough bread pieces
- 1/4 cup of marinara sauce or pizza sauce
- Pepperoni chunks
- Mozzarella cheese, diced or crushed

### Directions

- On one of the bread pieces, apply pizza sauce or marinara.
- Pepperoni slices should be added now.
- Place the second piece of bread over the pepperoni and mozzarella pieces.
- Put the sandwich inside a Panini machine or on a Foreman grill and cook until lightly browned.

## 6. CRAZY QUICK WHITE BEAN SALAD

Serving: 2

Preparation time: 10 min

Nutritional values: Calories-354kcal|Carbs-42g|Protein-14g|Fat-16g

### Ingredients

- 1 can of white beans
- 1 onion, red
- 4 oil-soaked sun-dried tomatoes
- 1 red bell pepper
- 2 tablespoons extra virgin olive oil
- 1 tablespoon of lemon juice
- 1 tiny handful of fresh parsley
- 1 tiny handful of fresh cilantro/coriander

### Directions

- Rinse & drain the beans.
- Cut the onion into tiny cubes.
- Wash the bell pepper and chop it into tiny pieces.
- Toss in the parsley and cilantro.
- Make tiny strips out of the dried tomatoes.
- Toss everything into a large mixing bowl, drizzle with olive oil, squeeze in some lemon juice, & season with salt and pepper.

## 7. THE QUINOA SALAD

Serving: 2

Preparation time: 20 min

Nutritional values: Calories-469kcal|Carbs-66g|Protein-18g|Fat-16g

## Ingredients

- Quinoa (3/4 cup)
- 1/4 papaya (approximately 300g; optionally, use mango)
- Peanuts, 1 handful
- Sesame seeds, 2 tablespoons
- 1 teaspoon of peanut oil (or extra virgin olive oil)
- Sugar snap peas, 1 handful
- 2 teaspoons coconut flakes
- 1 teaspoon of hot sauce (example, sriracha)
- 1/2 lemon (juiced; lime will also work)
- 1 fresh ginger thumb (grated)

## Directions

- Prepare the quinoa as directed on the package. Thump the stick of lemongrass on the worktop to "open it up," then toss it with a bit of salt into the quinoa.
- Discard the lemongrass once the quinoa is done.
- Scrape the mango/papaya, remove the seed(s), and chop into tiny cubes whilst quinoa is cooking. Toss them together in a mixing bowl.
- Coarsely crush the peanuts, then toast them with the seeds of sesame in a skillet over medium flame for 2 to 3 minutes (if not previously roasted). They, too, are tossed into the bowl.
- In the same pan, delicately sauté the snap peas for one minute with some oil (peanut) before tossing them into the bowl.
- Cut the red onion into thin slices and cut the (Thai) basil & mint leaves. Combine all of the ingredients, including the quinoa, in a mixing bowl. Finish with the juice of lemon, flakes of coconut, hot sauce, and shredded ginger. If you want to add garlic, now would be the time to do so.
- Enjoy.

# 8. VEGETABLE ORZO SOUP

Serving: 4

Preparation time: 30 min

Nutritional values: Calories-100kcal|Carbs-17g|Protein-3g|Fat-3g

## Ingredients

- 1 tbsp. extra virgin olive oil
- 1/2 medium chopped yellow onion
- 1 cup of celery, chopped (about 3 stalks)
- 1 cup of carrots, chopped (about 2-3 carrots)
- 1 large peeled & chopped bell pepper
- 2 chopped garlic cloves
- 1 can of chopped tomatoes (14.5 oz.)
- 6 c. vegetable stock
- 1 cup of orzo (whole wheat)
- 1 15.5-oz. cannellini bean (drained and washed) 1/2 lemon juice

## Directions

- In a wide saucepan over medium-low heat, heat the oil. Combine the onions, celery, carrots, as well as bell pepper in a large mixing bowl. Cook, stirring periodically, for 7 to 8 minutes. Sauté for 1 minute after adding the garlic and oregano.
- Bring to a simmer, stirring periodically, with the chopped tomatoes, stock, orzo, as well as cannellini beans. Lower the heat and continue to cook for 8 to 10 min, or unless the orzo is slightly done.
- Combine the lemon juice as well as parsley in a mixing bowl. To taste, sprinkle with salt and pepper.
- Serve in separate dishes with additional parsley on top. Enjoy!

# 9. VEGAN PEANUT NOODLES WITH CRISPY TOFU

Serving: 4

Preparation time: 35 min

Nutritional values: Calories-470kcal|Carbs-62g|Protein-23g|Fat-16g

## Ingredients

To make the peanut sauce

- 1/3 cup of peanut butter
- 3 tbsp. tamari or soy sauce
- Rice vinegar, 1 1/2 teaspoons
- 1 1/2 tbsp. maple syrup (or another liquid sweetener)
- 2 tbsp. sesame seed oil
- Optional: 1 tsp. chili powder

To make the noodle

- 1 1/4 oz. pressed & drained block super firm tofu
- 1/2 tsp. salt
- 1 tbsp. corn-starch
- Dry noodles of your choosing (8 ounces)
- 3 garlic cloves, chopped
- 3 cups of cabbage, shredded
- 1 julienned large carrot

## Directions

- Cook the noodles as per the package directions in a saucepan of boiling water. After cooking, drain & rinse beneath cold water.
- Meanwhile, prepare the peanut sauce by mixing all of the ingredients.
- 2 tsp. sesame oil, 1/3 of cup peanut butter, 3 tbsp. soy sauce, 1/2 tbsp. rice vinegar, 1/2 tbsp. maple syrup
- Mix the salt as well as corn starch in a mixing bowl. Place the tofu, including the corn-starch concoction, in a zip-top container. Toss until the tofu is well covered.
- In a large cast-iron / non-stick skillet, put a tablespoon or two of neutral-tasting oil over medium flame. Heat for 3-4 min on each side, or until lightly browned on most sides, in a coating of tofu. Place aside.
- Sauté garlic for 1 to 2 min with another 1/2 tbsp. of oil before putting cabbage & carrot. Sauté for 3-4 minutes, tossing periodically until the vegetables have cooked.
- Toss in the cooked noodles as well as tofu with the peanut sauce. Toss until all of the ingredients are thoroughly mixed. Taste it and, if necessary, add additional soy sauce. Take it off the heat, dish it up, and enjoy it!

# 10. THE VEGGIE KING

Serving: 1

Preparation time: 20 min

Nutritional values: Calories-415kcal|Carbs-83g|Protein-12g|Fat-7g

## Ingredients

- 1 potato, medium
- 1/2 zucchini
- 1/2 red bell pepper
- 1/4 cup of corn
- 1 tablespoon fajita seasoning (or 1 teaspoon cumin, 1 teaspoon chili powder, 1 teaspoon paprika, and 1/4 teaspoon salt)
- 1/8 cup of water

## Directions

- Microwave for 9 minutes the medium potato. A large potato will take 7 minutes to cook, whereas a tiny potato will take five minutes. Give 4 min for a potato, 3 min for a mid-sized potato,

& 2 min for a tiny potato when adding additional potatoes. If the microwave has low or high power, modify for considerably longer or shorter cooking times. Remember to poke the potatoes several times with a fork.

- Cut the zucchini as well as bell pepper into tiny pieces and cook for 6 min in the oil.

- While the vegetables are cooking, mix the seasonings (or the fajita seasonings and 1/8 cup of water. Stir it well before adding the corn for the final minute or so.

- Once the potato is ready, cut a wide groove in all directions in the core of it. Repeat the procedure in a diagonal direction.

- Using salt and black pepper, sprinkle the potato.

- Over the potato, pour the vegetable medley.

- Enjoy.

## 11. BESTVEGAN EGG SALAD SANDWICH

Serving: 6

Preparation time: 5 min

Nutritional values: Calories-190kcal|Carbs-4g|Protein-7g|Fat-15g

### Ingredients

- Firm Tofu, 16 ounces (water-packed)
- 1/2 cup of vegan mayo
- 3 tbsp. fresh chives, diced
- 1 tbsp. Yeast Flakes (Nutritional)
- 1 tsp. powdered onion
- 1 tsp. mustard (yellow)
- 1 tsp. black salt (Himalayan, Kala Namak, or Black Indian)
- 1/8 tsp. turmeric

### Directions

- To dry the Tofu, open the box and press firmly. To achieve the required texture, crush with a fork.

- Slice fresh chives & toss them in with the tofu.

- Mix together the rest of the ingredients thoroughly.

- Serve with gluten-free snacks and bread, or on bread or chips as preferred.

## 12. CHICKPEA SUMMER SALAD

Serving: 2

Preparation time: 15 min

Nutritional values: Calories-398kcal|Carbs-49g|Protein-17g|Fat-18g

### Ingredients

- 1 can of chickpeas (15.5-ounce chickpeas)
- One lime (zested & juiced)
- 1 pre-cooked beetroot
- 2 tablespoons seeds (mixed) (example, pumpkin and sunflower seeds)
- One orange (diced in filets)
- 1 teaspoon of hot sauce (example, sriracha)
- 1 garlic clove
- 1 tablespoon of water

### Directions

- Drain & rinse the chickpeas well. In a pan over medium heat, toast the seeds until aromatic (no oil needed).

- Place the parsley in a stick blender or mortar and chop it finely. Blend in the lime zest, juice of a lime, garlic, spicy sauce, extra virgin olive oil, salt, & pepper until smooth as well as green.

- Toss the chickpeas with the 'parsley dip' in a mixing bowl. Give it a nice toss ;), season with salt to taste, & serve.

- Chop the beetroot into great pieces, fillet the orange, and top the salad.

- Sprinkle additional capers to the center, toss in the seeds, and then enjoy.

## 13. AUTHENTIC MOROCCAN COUSCOUS SALAD

Serving: 2

Preparation time: 30 min

Nutritional values: Calories-424kcal|Carbs-83g|Protein-12g|Fat-16g

### Ingredients

- 3/4 cup of instant couscous (130g = 3/4 cups)
- 1/2 cup of water
- 1 teaspoon cumin
- 1 teaspoon ginger powder (fresh ginger is great as well. Finely diced it.)
- 1/2 pomegranate
- 1/2 zucchini (large)
- 1/2 red bell pepper
- 1/2 orange
- 1/4 oz. orange zest
- 1 fresh fig
- 1 tablespoon of raisins

### Directions

- Bring the water to a boil and pour it over the couscous in a wide serving dish.

- Cover with a dish towel or a cover and let aside for 5 minutes.

- Carefully loosen the couscous with a fork before adding the cumin, ginger powder, extra virgin olive oil, and paprika powder. You want it to be completely dry, with no large clumps.

- Remove the peel from the orange & shred the zest.

- Toss the orange, including the zest, into the salad after peeling and chopping it.

- Toss the seeds after deseeding the pomegranate

- Finely slice the zucchini & bell pepper. Toss both ingredients into the salad.

- If you happen to come upon a fig, cut it up and toss it in the salad.

- Wash & cut the parsley, as well as any other desired herbs, then add to the salad once more.

- Toss it around a bit.

- It's done. You've got a Moroccan couscous salad that's both fresh and tasty.

## 14. HEARTS OF PALM CRAB-STYLE SALAD

Serving: 2

Preparation time: 10 min

Nutritional values: Calories-16kcal|Carbs-1g|Protein-1g|Fat-1g

### Ingredients

- 1 lb. drained & sliced palm hearts
- 1 celery stalk, diced
- 1/2 cup of mayonnaise (vegan)
- 1/2 cup of chopped black olives
- 2 tbsp. chopped red onion
- 2 tbsp. flat-leaf parsley (Italian)
- 1 tsp. mustard, yellow
- 1/2 tsp. spice (Old Bay)

- 1/4 tsp. black pepper, crushed
- 1/8 tsp. powdered garlic

## Directions

- Combine all ingredients in a wide mixing bowl.
- To mix, carefully stir everything together. Season with salt and pepper to taste.
- Chill for at least one hour after covering.
- Serve chilled.

## 15. PEANUT NOODLE SALAD

Serving: 4

Preparation time: 15 min

Nutritional values: Calories-382kcal|Carbs-43g|Protein-21g|Fat-18g

## Ingredients

- 1/3 cup of peanut butter (creamy)
- 3 tablespoons tamari
- 3 tablespoons lime juice
- 1 tablespoon brown mustard (spicy)
- 3 tablespoons or Sriracha sauce (to taste)
- 1 tablespoon sesame oil, roasted
- 2 garlic cloves, minced
- 1 teaspoon grated fresh ginger
- 1 tablespoon sugar (or another sweetener of choice)

## Directions

- Bring a pot of salty water to a simmer, then add the spaghetti and cook for eight minutes. To chill cooked spaghetti, rinse it under chilled water.
- Combine the rest of the dressing ingredients in a mixing bowl and whisk until homogeneous; pour over chilled spaghetti & toss to coat. Refrigerate unless ready to eat.
- Top with your favourite garnishes just before dishing out.

## 16. WHITE BEAN SALAD

Serving: 2

Preparation time: 10 min

Nutritional values: Calories-357kcal|Carbs-45g|Protein-13g|Fat-15g

## Ingredients

- 1 medium can of white beans (about 285g)
- 2 c. lamb's lettuce (sometimes called corn salad)
- One orange
- 1 teaspoon mustard
- 1 teaspoon agave nectar (or honey)
- 1 tablespoon balsamic vinegar
- 1/2 teaspoon thyme (dried)
- 1 teaspoon of salt

## Directions

- Drain & rinse the white beans.
- Clean the lettuce from the lamb.
- The orange should be peeled and sliced.
- It's tossed into a bowl.
- In a mixing bowl, combine the mustard, agave nectar (or honey), olive oil, vinegar (balsamic), thyme, & salt. Then toss the salad with it.
- That's it.

## 17. MEDITERRANEAN CHICKPEA SALAD

Serving: 12

Preparation time: 45 min

Nutritional values: Calories-118kcal|Carbs-4g|Protein-1g|Fat-12g

### Ingredients

- 1 can (15 oz.) chickpeas, washed and drained
- 1 can (15 oz.) black beans, washed and drained
- 1 diced English cucumber
- 2 cups of half-sliced grape tomatoes
- 1/2 cup of red onion, chopped
- 1 cup of olives (green)
- 1/2 cup of black olives, diced

To make the dressing

- Red wine vinegar, 1/4 cup
- 1 tablespoon of lemon juice
- 1/2 tablespoon lemon zest
- 2 garlic cloves, chopped

### Directions

- Toss the chickpeas, black beans, diced cucumbers, diced tomatoes, diced olives, parsley, as well as mint in a large mixing bowl until thoroughly mixed. Place aside.
- Combine together the extra virgin olive oil, vinegar, juice of lemon, zest, as well as garlic in a mixing bowl. To taste, sprinkle with pepper & salt.
- In a glass dish, dressing is being drizzled over chickpea salad.
- Toss the salad with the dressing to mix it.
- Refrigerate the salad for thirty min after covering it.
- Serve right away, or keep in a sealed jar until ready to use.

## 18. RED PESTO PASTA

Serving: 2

Preparation time: 20 min

Nutritional values: Calories-395kcal|Carbs-45g|Protein-11g|Fat-20g

### Ingredients

- Sunflower seeds, 1 bunch
- Pasta (7 ounces)
- One onion
- 1 tablespoon extra-virgin olive oil
- 3-4 tablespoons red pesto
- 1 bunch spinach (1 bunch equals 50g or arugula)
- 1 cherry tomato bunch

### Directions

- Bring the pasta to a boil.
- In a skillet over medium heat, chop the onion and cook it with olive oil.
- While this is cooking, toast the seeds in a non-stick frying pan. Don't let them scorch! They'll just take a couple of minutes.
- Strain the cooked pasta and combine it with red pesto, spinach/arugula, and a large handful of chopped cherry tomatoes in a large skillet.
- If you want to make it creamier, add a few drops of water.
- Incorporate rennet-free cheddar cheese to taste, or keep it out for a vegan version based on your preferences.
- To serve, garnish with a few extra cherry tomatoes and a sprinkling of sunflower seeds.
- Enjoy.

# 19. BROCCOLI PESTO PASTA SALAD

Serving: 6

Preparation time: 30 min

Nutritional values: Calories-310kcal|Carbs-49g|Protein-10g|Fat-9g

## Ingredients

- Gluten-free rigatoni / spirals (12 oz.)
- Optional, paleo parmesan cheese

Pesto sauce with broccoli and basil

- Broccoli, 1 pound
- 1 cup basil leaves
- 1 cup spinach, baby
- 2 tiny garlic cloves, 0.2 ounces. garlic cloves
- 1/4 cup of pine nuts/walnuts
- Nutritional yeast, 3 tablespoons
- 1 cup of extra virgin olive oil
- Zest from half a lemon
- 2 tablespoons lemon juice, or to taste
- To taste, salt & pepper

## Directions

- Bring a wide saucepan of water (approximately 4 quarts) to a boil with 1.5 tablespoons coarse sea salt.

- Blanch the broccoli by dicing the base 1.5 inches of the broccoli stem. To remove the heads from the stem, make another cutting. Cut the lower portion of the stem using the knife's edge. Remove the rough & dense outer skin by slicing it off and discarding it. It should be diced into 2-inch pieces and then halved.

- Sauté the stems in hot water for approximately 10 minutes, or until completely soft. They'll be very tender. Drain them and set them aside. The stems will contribute to the creation of a smooth sauce.

- Cook the florets of broccoli for two min in boiling water. Maintain their crispness and tenderness. With a slotted spoon, remove the florets and rapidly wash them in iced water before draining.

- Put the same pan of water back to a boil for the pasta. Follow the package directions for cooking the pasta. To smooth the pesto sauce, keep 1/2 cup pasta water aside.

To make the pesto sauce, follow these steps

- Combine the florets of broccoli and stems with the remainder of the pesto sauce components, from basil to juice of lemon, in a high-powered blender or food processor. Blend until smooth, frothy, and brilliant green. Thin the sauce by adding 2 tablespoons of the saved pasta water at a time until it reaches the right consistency. To taste, sprinkle with pepper & salt.

- Toss the heated pasta with the gravy until everything is thoroughly combined. If preferred, season with additional salt or pepper. If desired, add a dollop of paleo parmesan (cashew nut) cheese. Serve hot or at ambient temperature.

# 20. LOW CARB HIGH TASTE ZOODLES

Serving: 2

Preparation time: 15 min

Nutritional values: Calories-364kcal|Carbs-15g|Protein-16g|Fat-30g

## Ingredients

- 1 zucchini, medium
- 1 cup of fresh basil
- 1 tablespoon pesto
- 1 cherry tomato, a handful
- 1 handful walnuts
- To taste with salt & pepper

- Feta cheese (1/4 cup)

**Directions**

- To prepare those beautiful zucchini noodles, often known as zoodles, use a spiralizer. If you don't have access to that miraculous device, you may just dice the zucchini.
- It's off into the skillet with some olive oil. Set the heat to medium.
- Toss in the cherry tomatoes, cut in half and add to the pan. Incorporate the walnuts as well.
- Toss it around a little. After 7 to 8 minutes, incorporate the pesto and mix it once again.
- Top the zoodles with basil leaves to complete
- It's done. Enjoy.

## 21. TURKISH LENTIL SALAD

Serving: 2

Preparation time: 7 min

Nutritional values: Calories-444kcal|Carbs-57g|Protein-19g|Fat-16g

**Ingredients**

- 1.5 cup of cooked brown lentils
- 1 onion, red
- 1 bunch fresh parsley
- 2 tablespoons extra virgin olive oil
- 1.5 tablespoon vinegar
- 1.5 tablespoons mustard
- 1 teaspoon of maple syrup
- 2 red bell peppers (green & red)
- Salt & pepper to taste

Optional

- 2 whole-grain bread slices

**Directions**

- Chop the bell pepper into tiny pieces and chop the onion. Combine the two ingredients in a salad bowl.
- Add the lentils & stir to combine.
- Smash up the parsley and toss it in with the 1.5 tbsp. vinegar, extra virgin olive oil, mustard, syrup (maple), salt, and pepper in a large mixing bowl.
- With a loaf of (whole grain) bread, serve the salad. Enjoy.

## 22. SMOKEY CHICKPEA LAVASH WRAP

Serving: 8

Preparation time: 30 min

Nutritional values: Calories-222kcal|Carbs-39g|Protein-10g|Fat-4g

**Ingredients**

- 3–4 tablespoons vegetable stock (low sodium)
- 3 garlic cloves, chopped
- 1 tiny red onion
- 1 tablespoon paprika (smoked)
- 1 teaspoon cumin
- Tomato paste, 3 tablespoons
- 1/4 teaspoon Himalayan pink salt
- 1/4 teaspoon of black pepper
- Apple cider vinegar, 1 tablespoon
- 1 teaspoon of maple syrup
- 1 tablespoon of hot sauce
- 1 cup of water
- 2 1/4 oz. cans of cooked chickpeas

- 3 cups of cooked chickpeas (rinsed and drained)

Wraps

- 8 wraps (lavash)
- 2 medium cucumbers, finely sliced
- 5 oz. of fresh spinach
- 1/2 cup of chopped green onions

## Directions

Sauté the chopped onion in 3-4 tablespoons vegetable stock in a large skillet over medium heat until tender and transparent.

In the same pan with the onions, incorporate chopped garlic, 1 tablespoon smoked paprika, 2 teaspoons cumin, 1/4 teaspoon salt, 1/4 teaspoon black pepper, & 3 tablespoons tomato paste. Toss it in and cook for another 2-3 minutes; it will be extremely aromatic.

In a large mixing bowl, combine 3 tablespoons lime juice, 1 tablespoon vinegar (apple cider), 1 tablespoon maple syrup, 1 tablespoon hot sauce, one cup of water, & 3 cups of cooked chickpeas. Stir everything together and simmer for 15 minutes or until the gravy thickens.

On a leveled surface, place a lavash wrap. Add 1 fistful of spinach on the wrap's left side (closest to you). Put approximately 1/2 cup of chickpeas beside the spinach. Spread a single layer of cucumbers to the right-side of the chickpeas. Apply pureed avocado or any other kind of sauce on the right-hand side of the lavash wrap (furthest from you); thus, it seals the wrap as you fold it. Green onions should be strewn over the top. Roll it up with the middle-folded in.

## 23. VEGAN BROCCOLI SALAD

Serving: 2

Preparation time: 13 min

Nutritional values: Calories-210kcal|Carbs-16g|Protein-8g|Fat-14g

## Ingredients

- Broccoli, 3 c. (roughly 1 bunch)
- 1 tablespoon extra-virgin olive oil
- Sesame seeds, 1 tablespoon
- 2 tablespoons peanuts
- 2 onions (spring) (sliced)
- 2 to 3 tablespoons water
- To make the sauce
- 1/5 cup of water
- 2 tablespoons soy sauce (dark)
- 1 tablespoon chili sauce (sweet)
- 1 tablespoon of vinegar
- 1 teaspoon of corn starch

## Directions

- Wash & dry the broccoli florets after cutting them into tiny pieces.

- Preheat a skillet over medium/high heat. Fill in one finger's width of water. And then there's the broccoli. On top, there's a cover. Sauté for three minutes at a minimum.

- Combine the corn starch and a little amount of cold water in a small mixing bowl. Cut the green onions as well as peanuts into slices.

- Remove the broccoli and set it aside. Fill the pan with water once more and let it heat up. Combine the soy sauce, extra virgin olive oil, sweet chili sauce, & vinegar in a mixing bowl. Add in the cornflour, lastly. Mix thoroughly.

- Return the broccoli to the saucepan. Combine sesame seeds, peanuts, as well as green onions in a bowl. Whisk for another thirty seconds, gradually.

- Season with salt to taste. Perhaps a little more vinegar.

- Done. Indulge right away or while it's cold.

# 24. ASIAN TOFU SALAD

Serving: 2

Preparation time: 20 min

Nutritional values: Calories-496kcal|Carbs-22g|Protein-24g|Fat-37g

## Ingredients

- Firm tofu, 14 ounces
- Radishes (1/2 bunch) 1 cup of bean sprouts
- 1/2 cucumber, medium
- 1 spinach, handful
- 1 medium pineapple can
- 1 tablespoon extra-virgin olive oil

To prepare the dressing

- 2 tablespoons extra virgin olive oil
- 1 tablespoon of maple syrup
- 1 teaspoon sriracha (or equivalent)
- 1/2 lime (juiced; lemon will work also)
- 1/2 chili pepper (jalapeno, for example)
- 1 handful of peanuts

## Directions

- Chop the tofu block into tiny cubes after pressing out some of the extra liquid. Put some oil in a skillet over medium heat before adding the tofu. Cook for fifteen min, or until lightly browned. Multitasking test: occasionally mix (and season with salt) while preparing the remainder of the salad. You can accomplish it, so go for it!
- After that, it's time to wash your vegetables!
- Cut the radishes into slices.
- Chop the cucumber in halves crosswise, scrape out the seeds with a tiny spoon, then cube the rest.
- Also, chop the pineapple into tiny pieces.
- Toss everything, including the spinach as well as bean sprouts, into a mixing bowl.
- Now comes the dressing.
- Mix the salad with olive oil (extra virgin), honey, sriracha, juice of a lime, salt, & pepper.
- In a different dish, put the tofu cubes. Toss a handful of them into each salad serving. (If you toss them into the salad straight away, they'll soon get mushy.)
- Cut the chile and coarsely smash or slice the peanuts for garnish. When serving, scatter them over the salad.
- Enjoy.

# 25. CHICKPEA CURRY

Serving: 3

Preparation time: 25 min

Nutritional values: Calories-465kcal|Carbs-65g|Protein-13g|Fat-17g

## Ingredients

- 1/2 cup of rice (basmati)
- 1 cup of water
- 2 onions
- 3 garlic cloves
- 1/2 lime
- 1–2 teaspoons curry paste
- 1 can of coconut milk (low fat)
- Chickpeas, 1 can
- 1–2 tablespoons soy sauce
- 2-3 midsize tomatoes (diced) or a handful of cherry tomatoes
- 1 teaspoon of maple syrup

## Directions

- Heat the rice, water, as well as a bit of salt to

a boil together. Take a look at the rice — after the water has reached a boil, cover it with a lid, turn down the heat

to low, and continue to cook for a further 8-10 minutes.

• Cut the onions, garlic, basil, as well as lime juice while this is going on.

• In a large skillet, combine the oil with onions and simmer over moderate flame until the onions are tender and become clear, approximately 5 minutes. Incorporate the garlic & cook for another minute.

• Mix in the curry paste & milk unless the curry is completely dissolved. Season with a bit of salt. Try the curry and add another teaspoon if you want it to be a bit stronger.

• Add the drained as well as rinsed chickpeas (and finely diced veg if using) then soy sauce, and simmer for five min on moderate flame, or until the curry reaches a boil. Reduce the heat quickly if it begins to burn.

• Cook the curry for a further two min after adding the diced tomatoes, basil, lime juice, as well as soy sauce.

• Taste, and if necessary, put another tablespoon of soy sauce as well as syrup and brown sugar. Stir it once more.

• By now, the rice must be done as well; fluff it with a fork.

• Dish out the curry and rice with alternative sides of papadoms & naan bread.

## 26. EASY CAPRESE SANDWICH

Serving: 1

Preparation time: 10 min

Nutritional values: Calories-210kcal|Carbs-41g|Protein-11g|Fat-1g

### Ingredients

- 2 slightly toasted pieces of bread
- 1 cup of assorted greens
- 1 thickly sliced heirloom tomato
- 2 vegan mozzarella cheese pieces
- 3-4 thinly chopped fresh basil leaves
- Balsamic glaze, 1 teaspoon

### Directions

• On a plate, layer 1 cup of assorted greens, 2 to 3 thick pieces of tomato, 2 pieces of vegan cheese, basil (fresh), as well as a sprinkle of balsamic glaze on one slice of gently toasted bread. Place the second slice of toasted bread on top and gently push it down. Before serving, cut in half.

• You may eat the sandwich fresh or warm it up in a Panini press for several minutes till the cheese melts.

## 27. SWEET & TANGY BUDDHA BOWL

Serving: 2

Preparation time: 25 min

Nutritional values: Calories-438kcal|Carbs-67g|Protein-16g|Fat-13g

### Ingredients

- 1/4 cup of raw quinoa
- Chickpeas, 1 can
- 2 handfuls (lamb's lettuce) corn salad
- 1 finely minced tiny red onion
- 2 dried figs

To make the dressing

- Mustard (1/2 tablespoon)
- 1 tablespoon extra-virgin olive oil

- 1.5 tablespoon maple syrup
- 1.5 tablespoon white vinegar
- 2 tablespoons of water

## Directions

- Prepare the quinoa as directed on the box.
- Cut the figs as well as chop the red onion
- Drain & rinse the chickpeas as well as salad.

To make the dressing

- Combine mustard, syrup (maple), white vinegar, extra virgin olive oil, salt, & pepper in a mixing bowl.
- Once the quinoa is done, combine everything in two separate bowls and spritz with the dressing.
- Enjoy.

## 28. CHINESE SESAME TOFU WITH GARLIC GINGER SAUCE

Serving: 2

Preparation time: 30 min

Nutritional values: Calories-249kcal|Carbs-15g|Protein-15g|Fat-15g

## Ingredients

Ginger & garlic sauce

- 4-ounce soy sauce (mild)
- 1-ounce hoisin sauce
- 3 ounces of sugar
- Pineapple juice, 6 ounces
- 4 ounces vegetable broth or water
- 7 large ginger slices, minced
- 7 garlic cloves, minced

- Slurry
- Corn starch, 1 tablespoon
- 1/4 cup of water

Others

- 1 firm tofu block, sliced into bite-size pieces
- Boiled broccoli as required
- Boiled cauliflower, as required
- Sesame seeds, gently toasted as required
- As required, dried or fresh chilies
- For frying, use vegetable oil as required.

## Directions

To make the sauce

- On medium flame, mix all ingredients in a double base saucepan. Bring to a simmer, then lower to a medium flame setting and let the contents simmer for ten min. Allow an hour for the ginger & garlic to soak in the concoction. After that, filter the liquid and keep it in an airtight jar in the fridge for up to two weeks.
- Before turning off the heat, pour the slurry into the pot and give it a few stirs. The sauce should completely cover the back of the spatula. Allow one hour for the ginger & garlic to soak in the concoction. After that, filter the liquid and keep it in an airtight jar in the fridge for up to two weeks.
- If the sauce thickens after being refrigerated or at any other time, dilute it down with 1 to 2 tablespoons of water and pineapple juice.

To make tofu

- Incorporate enough oil into a small frying pan and heat from 350F to 375F. Tofu cubes should be carefully placed. Working in small batches is recommended. For every batch, fry for around 3 to 5 minutes.
- Continue cooking until all of the tofu is done.

To make sesame tofu

- Add approximately 1 tablespoon vegetable oil to a double-bottom frying pan over medium-high heat, then several chunks of fried tofu as well as chilies. Shake the pan several times. Apply enough sauce to properly coat the tofu pieces. Turn the heat off.

- Eat sesame tofu right away with boiled rice and cooked broccoli & cauliflower. Enjoy.

## 29. VEGAN EGG MAYO SANDWICH

Serving: 4

Preparation time: 10 min

Nutritional values: Calories-319kcal|Carbs-33g|Protein-20g|Fat-11g

### Ingredients

- Silken tofu (150g)
- 280g tofu (firm)
- 2 tablespoons vegan mayonnaise
- 1/4 teaspoon kala namak
- 1 tablespoon of nutritional yeast
- 1/4 teaspoon powdered turmeric
- Pinch of black pepper (as per taste)
- A bunch of cress
- Bread, 8 pieces

### Directions

- In a mixing dish, crumble both kinds of tofu and combine them.
- Combine the rest of the ingredients (except the bread!) in a mixing bowl.
- Combine thoroughly.
- Butter the bread (vegan butter, of course) and put 1/4 of the mixture on each sandwich.
- Assemble the sandwich with the second piece of bread, incorporate the cress (if using), then take for lunch or tuck in.

## 30. HEALTHY MASHED SWEETPOTATO

Serving: 2

Preparation time: 25 min

Nutritional values: Calories-503kcal|Carbs-31g|Protein-2g|Fat-42g

### Ingredients

- 2 sweet potatoes, medium
- 5–6 tablespoons olive oil
- One chili pepper
- 2 garlic cloves
- 1 fresh ginger thumb
- 1/2 lime (juiced)
- 1 bunch fresh cilantro/coriander

### Directions

- Peel and cut the sweet potatoes, then place them in a wide saucepan of boiling, lightly salted water.
- Add the extra virgin olive oil to a medium skillet on medium heat while they're cooking. Take the garlic cloves & cut them in half. Strip the ginger & cut it into large chunks (they don't have to be perfect; you'll be removing it again shortly).
- Cut a large slit in the chili pepper, then add it, along with the garlic and ginger, to the oil. Allow it to absorb slowly by gradually frying whilst potatoes are frying. Make 4 incisions along with the chili rather than if you want your food to be a little hotter.
- Strain the potatoes when they're soft (zap them with a fork to see if they're done), then return them to the skillet.
- Scrape the ginger, garlic, & chili from the oil using a spoon, then ladle the oil (olive) into the po-

tatoes and mash everything together!

- Serve with a squeeze of lime juice and a sprinkling of coriander.

## 31. ASIAN STYLE CREAMY CORN SOUP

Serving: 3

Preparation time: 20 min

Nutritional values: Calories-541kcal|Carbs-101g|Protein-16g|Fat-16g

### Ingredients

- 3 sweet corn cans
- 2 onions
- 1 pepper (red)
- 2 garlic cloves
- 1 fresh ginger thumb (or 1 tablespoon ground ginger)
- 2 cups of vegetable stock (equivalent to 1/2 liters)
- 2 tablespoons extra virgin olive oil
- 2 handfuls of fresh cilantro/coriander
- 1 teaspoon of salt
- 1 tsp. pepper
- 2 lemongrass stalks (or 1 tablespoon lemongrass, ground)
- 1 tablespoon of lemon juice

### Directions

- Preheat the oven at 430 degrees Fahrenheit/220 degrees Celsius.
- Strain the sweetcorn, but save the can juice in a separate dish.
- Fill the baking pan with 1/3 cup of corn (without the liquid). Add additional oil, salt, & pepper to taste. Preheat the oven to 350°F and bake for ten min. Make sure the corn doesn't scorch by stirring it periodically.
- Meanwhile, heat the remaining tablespoon of oil in a skillet over moderate flame.
- Mince the onion & sauté (slowly cook) it.
- Toss the fresh ginger into the onion after peeling and chopping it. (Whether using dried ginger, wait a minute.) For a minute, stir everything together.
- Add the chopped garlic to the onion once it has been chopped. Stir for 30 to 60 seconds over low heat.
- Now is the time to bring the ground ginger (and, optionally, ground lemongrass) to the mixture and whisk for 30-60 seconds.
- Add the remaining two cans of corn (together with their water/moist/broth) and the liquor you put aside previously. Bring the veggie broth to a boil as well.
- Make tiny slits in the lemongrass and toss them to the soup, whether using fresh lemongrass. Alternatively, whack the lemongrass with a slotted spoon several times.
- Allow the soup to boil for approximately 10 minutes on low flame.
- Keep an eye on the roasted corn in the oven. In the meanwhile, chop the coriander and thinly slice the red pepper. If you don't like it hot, remove the seeds from the red pepper initially.
- Transfer the roasted corn, red pepper, as well as coriander to a bowl after it's done (browning, sizzling, & popping here and there). Mix everything up well.
- Take the soup off from the heat after 10 min and mix it (a mixer works well) until it's (sort of) smooth.
- Add a spoonful (or 2) of the corn-coriander and red pepper mixture to the soup before serving.

# 32. ONE POT HUMMUS PASTA

Serving: 2

Preparation time: 12 min

Nutritional values: Calories-994kcal|Carbs-171g|Protein-36g|Fat-19g

## Ingredients

- 1 3/4 cup of uncooked dry pasta
- 2/3 cup of pasta water
- 1 cup of homemade or store-bought vegan hummus
- 2 c. spinach, whole or coarsely chopped
- 20 sliced black olives, diced
- 8 sun-dried tomatoes, diced
- If required, a pinch of salt,

## Directions

- Cook the pasta as per the package directions, but remove it from the heat 1 minute before it's done. Dump off the majority of the water; however, keep some in the pot's base.

- Return the pasta & a small amount of boiling water to the stovetop over a moderate flame, and stir in the hummus. Bring to a boil, then reduce to a simmer for 1-2 minutes.

- In a large mixing bowl, combine the spinach, sun-dried tomatoes, & black olives. Remove from the heat after thoroughly mixing. Taste and season with salt if necessary. Serve right away.

# 33. ASIAN SLAW VEGAN WRAPS WITH CAULIFLOWER RICE

Serving: 8

Preparation time: 30 min

Nutritional values: Calories-197kcal|Carbs-25g|Protein-6g|Fat-5g

## Ingredients

- 1 tsp. of coconut oil
- 4 cups of riced cauliflower from 1 tiny head or half of a large head of cauliflower
- 1/2 tsp. of salt
- 4 cups coleslaw mix
- 1/4 cup of chopped cilantro
- If required, 8 gluten-free 10" tortilla wraps

Ingredients for the Dressing

- 2 tbsp. peanut butter, creamy
- 3 tbsp. soy sauce or tamari
- 3 tbsp. vinegar (rice)
- 2 tbsp. maple syrup
- Lime juice, 1 tbsp. a lime (about half a lime)
- 1/2 tsp. of garlic powder
- 1/2 tsp. sriracha (optional)

## Directions

- Chop the cauliflower into rice texture in a stick blender or with a vegetable bullet. If you're going to use a stick blender, do smaller batches so you don't over-process the cauliflower. It should not be pureed.

- In a large pan, warm the coconut oil over medium flame until it is hot. After that, incorporate the cauliflower rice & season with salt. Cook for approximately 10 minutes, stirring periodically, or until gently browned. Place aside.

- In the meanwhile, combine the slaw as well as cilantro in a large mixing bowl and leave aside while you make the dressing.

- In a small mixing bowl, combine all of the dressing ingredients and stir well to incorporate the peanut butter. Then drizzle the vinaigrette over the slaw & toss to combine.

- Distribute the cauliflower rice & prepared slaw evenly among the eight wraps. In the middle of each wrap, place 2 tbsp. of cauliflower rice & 3 tbsp. of slaw. Tuck the tortilla wrap's edges in first, then cover the top & bottom to prevent anything from spilling out the sides. If the wraps are too full, they will be hard to close.

- Optional, but strongly suggested: Lightly cook the wraps, turned side down, for approximately 2 minutes in a panini machine or grill with a cover. This will assist in keeping your wraps together while also giving them nice grill marks.

- Cut the wraps in halves or serve them whole. Enjoy.

## 34. FABULOUS FALAFEL SALAD WITH FAKE TAHINI SAUCE

Serving: 2

Preparation time: 25 min

Nutritional values: Calories-591kcal|Carbs-70g|Protein-17g|Fat-25g

### Ingredients

- 6.5 ounce Falafel (about 180g/6.5 ounce falafel mix)
- 1/2 cucumber
- 1/2 onion (red)
- 8 tomatoes, cherry
- Two carrots
- 2 tablespoons extra virgin olive oil

For the dressing

- Peanut butter, 2 tablespoons
- Lemon juice, 2 tablespoons
- 1 teaspoon of maple syrup
- 1/2 teaspoon salt
- 1/5 cup of warm water (1/5 cup equals 50ml)

### Directions

- Cook the falafel as directed on the box. While cooking, don't smack them around too much in the skillet, or they'll break apart. Rather, stir & cook each side gently.

- To make the salad, finely slice the cucumber, cut the red onion, and a quarter or half the tomatoes. Shred the carrots and combine everything.

- To make the sauce, thoroughly combine all of the ingredients in a mixing bowl.

- Toss the salad on a plate with the falafel & sauce drizzled on top. Done.

## 35. VEGAN TUNA SALAD

Serving: 4

Preparation time: 15 min

Nutritional values: Calories-428kcal|Carbs-50g|Protein-16g|Fat-19g

### Ingredients

- Chickpeas, 1 can (drained & rinsed)
- Mustard (1 tablespoon)
- 1 tablespoon of lemon juice
- 2 tablespoons soy sauce
- 4 tablespoons extra virgin olive oil
- 1/2 red bell pepper
- 4 tiny gherkins, pickled
- 2 onions (spring)

### Directions

- Drain & rinse the chickpeas.

- In a blender or food processor, combine the chickpeas, soy sauce, extra virgin olive oil, mustard, as well as lemon juice. Blend until the mixture is almost completely smooth.

- Slice the green onions & bell pepper into small pieces. In a food processor, combine them with the gherkins. This time, blend the salad slightly to give it some texture (it shouldn't be an extreme sauce).

- Try it and add additional mustard & lemon juice if you want it to be a bit stronger.
- Put on thick toast with a parsley garnish.

## 36. VEGETABLE BIRYANI

Serving: 6

Preparation time: 45 min

Nutritional values: Calories-385kcal|Carbs-73g|Protein-8g|Fat-7g

### Ingredients

- 2 cups of basmati rice, white
- 2 tbsp. extra virgin olive oil
- 1 finely sliced medium onion
- 1 coarsely chopped red bell pepper
- 1 cup carrots, chopped
- 4 rough minced garlic cloves
- 2 tsp. grated fresh ginger (or ginger paste)
- 1 tbsp. cumin powder
- 1 tbsp. coriander powder
- 1 tsp. chili powder
- 1 pinch of cinnamon (or 1 stick of cinnamon)
- A half teaspoon of cardamom (or 3 ground cardamom pods)
- 1/2 tsp. turmeric powder
- Bay leaves (two)
- 4 c. vegetable stock (or chicken broth)
- 3/4 tsp. salt, plus more as desired
- 1 can of washed and drained chickpeas
- Half cup of raisins
- 1/4 cup of cashews with diced parsley or cilantro for garnish
- Serve with a vegan-friendly Cilantro Mint Chutney.

### Directions

- While you prepare the ingredients, soak the rice in a dish of boiling water.
- Heat the oil in a wide skillet or small Dutch oven over moderate flame. Incorporate the onion & cook, often stirring, for five min, or until soft and golden. Reduce to moderate flame, add the vegetables, garlic, and ginger, and cook for 4-5 minutes. Take off & set aside 1 cup of the mixture.
- Toss in the spices as well as bay leaf for one min to toast the spices. Strain the rice and combine it with the vegetable stock and salt in a mixing bowl.
- Cover with chickpeas, raisins, as well as the reserved cup of vegetables. Bring to a boil over medium heat, then reduce to a low flame. Wrap the saucepan with a soft hand towel, then put the lid on top of it, bringing the cloth's four corners up & over the cover. This will strengthen the seal and enable the steam to escape, enabling the rice to boil faster and more evenly.
- Simmer for 20 to 30 minutes on low heat, or unless the rice has absorbed all of the liquid.
- Prepare the Mint Chutney (cilantro) while it's boiling.
- Remove the Vegetarian Biryani from the pan and fluff with a fork. Toss in the roasted cashews and cilantro to finish. Serve with chutney, if desired.

## 37. WHOLE ROASTED CAULIFLOWER WITH TAHINI SAUCE

Serving: 4

Preparation time: 1 hr. 40 min

Nutritional values: Calories-127kcal|Carbs-12g|Protein-5g|Fat-8g

## Ingredients

- 1 large cauliflower (whole!)
- 2 tbsp. extra virgin olive oil halved
- 1/2 tsp. of salt
- 1 tbsp. zaatar (or dukkah!) spice (Alternatively, combine coriander, cumin, as well as optional sumac)
- 1 cup of water
- 1 tahini sauce batch
- Top with extra Aleppo chili flakes & spritz with this additional Tahini sauce! Sprinkle with fresh herbs – parsley, dill, and perhaps mint

## Directions

- Preheat the oven to 425 degrees Fahrenheit.
- Chop the cauliflower, either by removing the stem (which is simpler) or by clipping & slicing the base, so it sticks up straight.
- Put it in a Dutch oven or perhaps an oven-safe skillet. Pour 1 tbsp. oil over the cauliflower & season with salt as well as Zaatar spice to taste. Add 1 cup of water to the pan's bottom.
- Cover firmly with the cover or foil & bake for 45 to 60 minutes, or until soft when poked with a knife all the way through. Shorter cauliflower heads might take 45 minutes to cook, while bigger ones might take up to 60 minutes.
- Remove the cover or foil with care, keeping in view the hot steam (this would burn!). Drizzle with some more olive oil and return to the oven for another 30 minutes, turning halfway through. It should be thoroughly brown at this stage, but if it isn't, continue grilling until it is... no yellow cauliflowers here!!!
- Take out from the oven and top with additional za'atar, fresh herbs, & optional Aleppo chili flakes. Pour the sauce (tahini) over the entire thing directly in the skillet, or chop it up into pieces like a cake & serve the sauce on the platter.
- Enjoy.

# 38. FRANKIES

Serving: 4

Preparation time: 1 hr.

Nutritional values: Calories-490kcal|Carbs-77g|Protein-14g|Fat-15g

## Ingredients

- 16 oz. chopped up baby potatoes
- 1 tbsp. ghee, olive oil, or coconut oil, plus more to flavor
- 3/4 tsp. kosher salt
- 2–3 tsp. curry powder (yellow)
- 1 tsp. onion powder/garlic powder, granulated

For filling of roasted cauliflower & chickpeas

- 1 cauliflower head, chopped into tiny florets
- 1 can of chickpeas, washed and well-drained
- 1–2 tbsp. extra virgin olive oil
- 1 1/2 tablespoons salt (kosher)
- 1 tbsp. coriander
- 1 tbsp. cumin, a hefty sprinkle of chili flakes
- 1 tsp. fennel seed, whole
- 1 tsp. coriander seed, whole

For burrito Fixin's

- 4 extra-large whole-grain tortillas – alternatively use gluten-free wraps

alternatively tortillas, or make GF bowls with the mashed potatoes & additional spinach as the base.

- Baby spinach, 2 handfuls
- Cilantro Mint Chutney (a few tbsp.)

- Instant Pickled Onions (a few tbsp.)

**Directions**

- Preheat the oven to 425 degrees Fahrenheit.

- Begin with the potatoes: Peel & cut the potatoes, then put them in a large skillet with enough water to cover them & cook until very soft, approximately 15-20 minutes. Concurrently.

- Vegetables to roast: Chop the cauliflower into tiny florets and put them on a baking sheet coated with parchment paper (to one side). On the opposite side, put the drained chickpeas. Pour olive oil over both. Toss the cauliflower as well as chickpeas with the seasonings & salt, making sure they're thoroughly coated. Bake for 20-30 min (tossing halfway around) or unless cauliflower is cooked in the oven.

- Sauce: Fill jars with the delicious Cilantro Mint Chutney & instant pickled red onions. Each one takes approximately 5-10 minutes.

- Curried potatoes: Strain the potatoes when they are extremely soft, but save approximately 1 cup of boiling water. Return the potatoes to the saucepan and mash with part of the lukewarm water (begin with 14-12 cups), salt, seasonings, plus ghee (or oil) to mix until smooth. If required, add additional boiling water to get a loose, runny mash. Wipe the sides of the container. Stir everything together well. Taste. For additional richness, feel free to incorporate additional ghee/oil as needed. Keep warm by covering.

- Assemble: Once the roasted vegetables are done, Warm the tortillas until soft and malleable in the oven, over a stove, or on a grill. Layer the curried potatoes on top, then add the chickpeas and cauliflower, being careful to scrape up any of the whole seasonings that have fallen to the sides of the

- Make a burrito out of a bunch of spinach leaves, several tsp. of cilantro mint chutney, as well as some pickled onions. Serve warm or heat it up in the oven unless ready to serve. For on-the-go dinners, you can also freeze and reheat.

- Enjoy.

# 39. SZECHUAN EGGPLANT

Serving: 4

Preparation time: 45 min

Nutritional values: Calories-323kcal|Carbs-29g|Protein-6g|Fat-21g

## Ingredients

- 1 1/2-pound Japanese eggplant (approximately 4 x 10-inch eggplants)
- 2 tsp. salt
- 2 tsp. salt
- 2–4 tbsp. peanut oil
- 2 tbsp. corn-starch
- 4 garlic cloves, coarsely chopped
- 2 tablespoons ginger, coarsely chopped
- 5–10 dried red chills

For Szechuan sauce

- 1 tsp. peppercorns (Szechuan)
- 1/4 cup of soy sauce (or soy sauce with reduced sodium)
- 1 tbsp. chili paste (garlic) (or 1 tsp. chili flakes)
- 1 tbsp. sesame seed oil
- 1 tbsp. vinegar (rice)
- 1 tbsp. cooking wine, Chinese (or mirin)
- 3 tbsp. sugar
- A half tsp. of five-spice
- Serve with scallions and toasted peanuts for a crunchier rendition of this Peanut Chili.

## Directions

- Chop eggplant into half-moons / bite-sized chunks that are 1/2 inch thick. Place in a large mixing bowl with 2 tsp. salt and fill with water. Allow for 20-30 minutes of resting time after covering with a plate.

- Meanwhile, prepare the Szechuan Sauce by chopping the garlic & ginger.

- To prepare the Szechuan sauce, follow these steps: In a dry pan over medium heat, sauté the (Szechuan) peppercorns for 1 to 2 minutes. Grind. In a separate bowl, mix together the rest of the ingredients (soy sauce, chili paste, oil, rice vinegar, cooking wine, sugar, & five spices). Place beside the stove.

- Strain the eggplant & rinse it before patting it dry with a napkin. Combine the corn starch and toss well.

- In an extra-large saucepan, heat 1-2 tbsp. oil over the moderate flame in two batches. Half of the eggplant should be spread out. Bide your time but don't hurry this stage if you really want all sides to be golden as well as the insides to be cooked thoroughly. Allow one side to brown before flipping with tongs. Every batch would take approximately 10 minutes to complete. Remove the eggplant and set it aside.

- Incorporate 1 tablespoon additional oil into the pan and cook the ginger & garlic for two min over a moderate flame, stirring constantly. Switch on the fan & stir for one minute after adding the dry chilies. Stir the Szechuan sauce to a boil in the skillet for 20 seconds. Return the eggplant to the saucepan and stir gently for 1 min. If it appears to be too dry, add a spoonful of water to soften it up.

- Garnish with scallions as well as optional peanuts on a serving platter.

- Serve with rice, rice (cauliflower), black rice, as well as rice noodles as a side dish.

## 40. VEGAN ALFREDO

Serving: 2

Preparation time: 30 min

Nutritional values: Calories-503kcal|Carbs-64g|Protein-21g|Fat-21g

### Ingredients

- 1–2 tbsp. extra virgin olive oil
- 1/2 onion, white
- 4 garlic cloves, fat
- 1/2 cup soaked uncooked cashews (or hemp seeds)
- 1 cup of vegetable broth
- Nutritional yeast, 2 tbsp.
- 1/2 tsp. miso paste (white)
- 1/8 tsp. nutmeg
- 1/2 tsp. salt
- 5 oz. dried pasta (cook according to package instructions)
- 1 cup peas, fresh
- 8 oz. sautéed mushrooms, or try roasted mushrooms

### Directions

- Bring a large pot of salted water to a simmer and boil pasta as per package instructions. Feel free to add frozen or fresh peas to the water of pasta during the final minute of cooking.

- To make Alfredo sauce, follow these steps: Sauté onion & garlic in oil over medium-low heat until brown and soft. Combine it with cashews, vegetable broth, yeast, miso, salt, and nutmeg in a processor. Pulse until the mixture is creamy & smooth.

- Prepare the mushrooms by sautéing or smoking them. Heat the oil in a pan over medium heat if sautéing. Sprinkle with salt & fry mushrooms for 6-7 minutes, until brown and soft.

- Drain the pasta, mix with the sauce of Alfredo in a wide skillet, and gradually reheat over low flame. Stir in the mushrooms to cover.

- Divide the mixture into two bowls.

- Serve with the zest of lemon, pepper, chili flakes, as well as chopped parsley as garnish.

# 41. VEGAN BROCCOLI CHEDDAR JALAPENO SOUP

Serving: 5

Preparation time: 38 min

Nutritional values: Calories-267kcal|Carbs-24g|Protein-8g|Fat-18g

## Ingredients

- 2 tbsp. extra virgin olive oil
- 1 large chopped onion
- 1 to 2 poblano peppers, chopped 1 jalapeño, chopped finely 4 to 6 garlic cloves, fat, roughly diced
- 7 cups of broccoli, chopped into bite-size florets (approximately 1– 1 1/4 lb.; stems are OK if thinly sliced)
- 4 cups of vegetable or chicken stock (or 4 cups of water plus 1 tbsp. vegetable base "Better than Bouillon")
- 1 cup of water
- 1 leaf of bay
- 1 tsp. kosher salt
- 1 tsp. coriander, chopped
- 1 tsp. oregano
- 1/2 tsp. black pepper
- 3/4 cup of raw cashews or hemp hearts (soaked or simmering)
- Nutritional yeast (about 2–3 tbsp.)
- 1 to 2 large bunch of baby spinach

## Directions

- In a large saucepan, add the oil over a medium flame, the onion, garlic, poblanos, & jalapeño, stirring periodically, for approximately 5 minutes, or until golden.

- Combine the broccoli, stock, water, leaf (bay), coriander, dried oregano, salt, as well as pepper in a large mixing bowl. The liquid ought to be enough to cover the vegetables. Cover, bring to a simmer, then reduce heat to low and cook until broccoli is cooked, approximately 10-12 minutes. Remove the bay leaf & turn down the heat.

- BLEND: In a processor, combine about 1 cup of broccoli as well as 1 cup of stock. Allow 5 minutes for cooling. Combine the cashews plus 2 tbsp. nutritional yeast in a mixing bowl.

- To avoid a blender "outburst," cover securely with mixer lid as well as kitchen towel, then push it down firmly while starting the machine. Blend until the mixture is velvety smooth.

- Add another cup of broccoli and another cup of broth. Blend until ultra-smooth once more.

- Add 1-2 large fistfuls of raw baby spinach to the mixer for an additional vivid "green" color, and mix until creamy and completely integrated.

- Return to the broccoli soup saucepan, stir, and heat gradually over low flame, being cautious not to simmer or boil for too long; otherwise, the beautiful bright green color will fade.

- Check for salt, heat, especially acidity. If desired, add a splash of lime, additional red pepper flakes, or more pepper. Add additional tbsp. of nutritional yeast for a "cheesier" taste.

- Serve with fresh cilantro, diced scallions, or a slice of lime as a garnish.

# 42. BUTTERNUT SQUASH RISOTTO

Serving: 5

Preparation time: 30 min

Nutritional values: Calories-321kcal|Carbs-48g|Protein-8g|Fat-10g

## Ingredients

- Olive oil, 2 tbsp. (or butter)
- 2 cups of leeks, chopped

- 4 rough sliced garlic cloves
- 8 crushed sage leaves
- 1 cup of Arborio rice / Spanish short-grain rice (Bomba)
- 2 heaped cups of diced butternut squash
- 1/4 cup of white wine
- 2 cups broth (vegetable or chicken) or stock (or water & one tsp. or piece of veggie bouillon)
- A half teaspoon of salt
- White pepper, 1/8 tsp. (or substitute with black pepper as per taste)
- Nutmeg (1/2 tsp.)
- 2-3 handfuls of diced kale or baby spinach

### Directions

- Cut the rings of leeks after slicing & washing them
- Configure the Instant Pot to "Sauté" mode.
- Inside the instant pot, heat the oil, then add the washed leeks and whisk for two min. Stir in the garlic, sage, and then rice for 2 minutes.
- Toss in the butternut squash for a few minutes until a little browning appears on the base of the pot.
- Scrounge up the browned pieces with a wooden spoon after adding the wine. Allow the wine to simmer off completely, approximately 2-3 minutes. Incorporate the stock/broth into the pot. Scrape up any remaining browned pieces. Stir in the salt, pepper, as well as nutmeg until well combined.
- Lock the instant pot, then cook for 6 minutes at increased speed. Allow for spontaneous release for five min before manually releasing.
- You may prepare the leek oil or maple-glazed pecans, whereas the pot is heating up.
- If desired, incorporate the spinach plus cheese or butter to the risotto, or keep them out entirely. The butternut will give a fresh smoothness to the risotto as it breaks down.
- Optional garnishes include leek oil as well as maple-glazed pecans.

## 43. VEGAN TACOS WITH SMOKY CHIPOTLE PORTOBELLOS

Serving: 2-3

Preparation time: 30 min

Nutritional values: Calories-307kcal|Carbs-41g|Protein-9g|Fat-11g

### Ingredients

- 2 portobello mushrooms, extremely large
- 1 red bell pepper, chopped
- 1/2 onion (optional)

For marination

- 1 tablespoon of olive oil
- 2 tbsp. Chipotle in Adobo Sauce (canned)
- 1 garlic clove, chopped (or 1/2 tsp. garlic granules)
- 1/2 tsp. cumin
- 1/2 tsp. coriander
- a pinch of salt
- 4 heated tortillas
- 1 can of warmed refried black beans

### Directions

- Preheat the oven to 425 degrees Fahrenheit.
- Cut the portobellos (Mushroom) into half-inch thick pieces and the bell pepper into half-inch thick strands. Cut onion into half-inch thick lobes or half-moons if using.
- Place everything on a parchment-lined sheet pan and whisk together the marinade ingre-

dients in a small dish.

- Spread the marinade generously on all sides of the mushrooms, then gently on the residual red bell pepper & onion. Season the portobellos with salt and pepper. Bake for twenty minutes, or until fork-tender portobellos.

- Fry the beans and prepare any extra toppings while this is cooking. It takes approximately 10 minutes to prepare both pickled onions as well as vegan cilantro crema. Alternatively, avocado slices may be used.

- Heat the tortillas (over a gas burner on the stovetop or in a toaster) and thoroughly spread with the fried black beans while ready to serve. Toss the tortillas with the chipotle portobellos, peppers, & onions (if using). Garnish with Cilantro, Poblano (Salsa), or avocado, fresh cilantro, plus pickled onions, if desired.

# 44. VEGAN SPAGHETTI AND BEETBALLS

Serving: 6

Preparation time: 1 hr. 10 min

Nutritional values: Calories-668kcal|Carbs-82g|Protein-22g|Fat-29g

## Ingredients

- 1 chopped yellow onion
- 2 chopped medium garlic cloves
- 1 medium beet, coarsely cut into 1/2-inch pieces (5oz or approximately 1 cup full)
- 1 medium carrot, coarsely cut into 1/2-inch pieces (2 1/2 ounces or 1/2 cup)
- 1 tbsp. paste of tomato
- 1 tbsp. vegan Worcestershire sauce
- nutritional yeast, 1/8 cup
- 1 tsp. psyllium powder
- 1 cup (3 ounces) roasted walnuts
- fresh basil leaves, 1 cup (1 ounce)
- 15-ounce drained black bean can
- 3 1/2 cup of tomato sauce
- 2 tbsp. chopped garlic cloves
- Optional: 1/8–1/4 tsp. red pepper flakes
- 28 ounce can of whole tomatoes & juices
- 1/2 cup of walnuts sprinkled vegan cheesy
- Hemp seed, 1/4 cup
- nutritional yeast, 1/4 cup
- 16 oz. dried linguini or spaghetti

## Directions

- Make the beet-balls according to the instructions.

- Preheat the oven at 335 degrees Fahrenheit.

- For ten min, roast raw walnuts. Allow cooling.

- Fry onion & garlic in a pan over moderate heat for approximately 10 minutes, or until tender and gently caramelized. Allow it cool for a few minutes.

- Combine the cooled walnuts & basil leaves in a stick blender. Pulse the mixture until it resembles granular sand. Set aside the walnut mixture from the processor.

- Put the cooled caramelized onion/garlic combination, raw beet pieces, raw carrot pieces, oregano (dried), salt, pepper, the paste of tomato, Worcestershire, nutritional yeast, as well as psyllium in the same high-speed blender until the concoction is just thoroughly minced, allowing for some texture.

- Toss in the black beans with the beets. Pulse three to four times.

- After that, toss in the walnuts. Pulse a few times. Just enough to take everything into account. There will be a lot of moisture in the mixture. It is possible to firm them up by refrigerating them for thirty min, although it is not required.

- Scoop the mixture onto a baking sheet. Preheat oven to 335°F and bake for 40 minutes. Leave to cool on the skillet after removing from the oven.
- Boil the pasta according to the package instructions.

Preparing the Tomato Sauce

- In a large skillet, heat the olive oil. Stir in the chopped garlic & red pepper flakes for approximately 3-5 minutes, or until gently toasted.
- Toss in the tomatoes with a spatula to split them up. Season with oregano as well as salt.
- Cook for twenty minutes at a low boil, tossing and pounding the tomatoes every four min or so. As the sauce simmer, it will thicken.
- Remove from heat a few moments before adding fresh basil leaves.
- Sprinkle on the "Cheesy"
- Pulse walnuts, seeds of hemp, nutritional yeast, & salt in a food processor until combined.
- In a saucepan over medium heat, toast the almonds.
- Stir continuously for approximately 5 minutes or until the toasted fragrance emerges. This sprinkle will last a few weeks in the fridge. It freezes well.
- Toss the prepared pasta with the sauce, then garnish with a few beetballs as well as a "cheesy sprinkle" to finish.

## 45. COCONUT MILLET BOWL WITH BERBERE SPICED SQUASH & CHICKPEAS

Serving: 4

Preparation time: 50 min

Nutritional values: Calories-641kcal|Carbs-75g|Protein-15g|Fat-27g

## Ingredients

For roasting sheet pan
- 2 tbsp. Berbere seasoning
- Avocado oil (two tbsp.)
- Water, 2 tbsp.
- 1 1/2-pounds kabocha squash, cut into 3/4" slices
- 1 1/2 cups of cooked chickpeas (15 ounces can chickpeas, drained)
- 2 shallots, scraped and diced thickly

For coconut millet
- millet, 1 cup
- 1 cup of coconut milk (not light!) from a 15-ounce can divide
- 1 tbsp. coconut oil 1 1/2 cups of water
- ¼ tsp. of turmeric
- Salt (1/4 tsp.)

For sauce
- coconut cream (1/2 cup)
- 1/4 cup of lime juice (equivalent to 1–2 limes)
- 1 lime's zest (about 1 tsp.)
- ¼ tsp. of salt
- 1 tsp. of honey
- 1/2 cup scraped & seeded cucumber pieces
- 1 tsp. fresh ginger shredded (or a few thin pieces)
- 1/2 cup of fresh cilantro, stems and leaves coarsely chopped
- 1/4 cup coarsely diced fresh mint leaves
- 3 cups of spinach (fresh)

## Directions

- Preheat the oven at 400 degrees Fahrenheit.

To prepare the berbere paste

- Combine all the ingredients in a mixing bowl.
- In a dish, combine berbere, oil, as well as water; put away for ten min to hydrate.
- prepare the millet
- Set aside a half cup of the dense cream portion of the coconut milk.
- In a skillet, add the residual coconut milk, water, powder of turmeric, as well as salt to a boil. Bring the coconut oil plus millet to a moderate boil, then reduce to low heat and cover for fifteen min. Without taking the lid off. Cover (no peeking!) and set aside. Turn off the heat and set it aside for another 10 minutes.

To make a sheet pan roast

- Place the squash, shallots, as well as chickpeas on a parchment-lined sheet pan. Distribute berbere paste generously using a brush. Season with salt and pepper and bake for thirty min, or unless everything is done and roasted to perfection.
- Season with salt and pepper and bake for thirty min, or unless everything is done and roasted to perfection.

To prepare drizzle

- Preserve the coconut cream, then blend it with the lime juice and zest of lime, salt, honey, diced cucumber, and ginger until creamy. Pulse in the cilantro as well as mint for a few seconds more, just long enough to separate the herbs but leave some bits and flecks.
- Arrange the vegetables over the heated millet in the bowls. Pour the sauce over the fresh spinach.
- The toasted coconut should be sprinkled on top.

## 46. VEGAN TIKKA MASALA

Serving: 4

Preparation time: 30 min

Nutritional values: Calories-210kcal|Carbs-17g|Protein-4g|Fat-16g

### Ingredients

- Coconut oil, olive oil, or ghee, 1–2 tbsp.
- 1 extremely-large shallot (or half red onion) – diced
- 1 tbsp. ginger, diced
- 4 garlic cloves, coarsely chopped
- 1 tsp. cumin powder
- 1 tsp. coriander, chopped
- 1 tsp. turmeric powder
- 1/2 tsp. paprika (red chili powder)
- 1 tsp. curry powder (garam masala)
- 1 1/2 cups of chopped tomatoes
- 1 can of full-fat coconut milk
- 1 large, chopped red bell pepper
- 1 cauliflower head, cut into 1-inch chunks or tiny florets
- 1 zucchini, sliced into half-moons 1 inch thick (or quarters)
- lemon squeeze

### Directions

- In a large heavy-bottomed saucepan or Dutch oven, heat the oil over moderate flame.
- Reduce heat to medium-low to avoid burning the shallot, ginger, as well as garlic, and cook, constantly turning for approximately 3 minutes until aromatic and golden. To improve the taste of the spices, seeds, & salt, gently toast them while stirring for 1-2 minutes.
- Cook for another 2 minutes, until the chopped tomato has softened, then pour the coconut milk & mix thoroughly before bringing to a boil. Stir in the cauliflower, diced red bell pepper, & zucchini, then cover and cook for 10-12 minutes on

low flame. Examine the cauliflower for softness; if not, continue to cook uncovered until optimum tenderness is achieved

• Taste and season with lemon juice if desired. If required, season with additional salt. Add cayenne pepper to taste if you prefer it spicy.

• Warm through by gently folding in the crunchy tofu, grilled paneer, or chickpeas.

• Put in bowls with basmati rice as well as naan and cilantro on top.

## 47. CRISPY QUINOA CAKES WITH TOMATO CHICKPEA RELISH

Serving: 4

Preparation time: 1 hr. 15 min

Nutritional values: Calories-388kcal|Carbs-48g|Protein-12g|Fat-17g

### Ingredients

For quinoa cakes

- 2 cups of water
- 1 cup of white quinoa, washed and drained
- 2 tsp. extra virgin olive oil
- 1 teaspoon cumin
- 1 tsp. garlic powder, granulated
- kosher salt (1/2 teaspoon)
- 1/2 tsp. Provence herbs

For chickpea relish with fresh tomatoes

- 2 cups half-sliced cherry/grape tomatoes
- 1 cup chopped cucumber
- 1/4 cup of fresh basil (or flat-leaf parsley, dill, mint, or a combination) chopped
- 1/4 cup of scallions, diced
- 1/2 cup of chickpeas, boiled
- 3 tbsp. extra virgin olive oil
- 3 tbsp. balsamic vinegar
- 1/4 teaspoon of salt

### Directions

• Add washed white quinoa, salt, powder of garlic, cumin, herbs (dried), and olive oil to a medium saucepan over high temperature and mix to combine. Bring the water to a boil. Cover, reduce heat to low, then cook for 20 minutes. Set a timer.

• Prepare the (Tomato Chickpea) Relish, although the quinoa is boiling by mixing all of the components together in a mixing bowl.

• Make sure all of the liquid has been absorbed by the quinoa. If not, cover and simmer for another 5 minutes, or until steam holes form (this typically takes me 25 minutes), as well as the quinoa, has absorbed all of the water and seems pretty dry.) Quinoa must be dry but not watery. Be patient since every stove is different.

• Although the quinoa is still warm, aggressively mix it with a fork for 1 minute or until the tiny grains begin to break away. To get the quinoa to adhere, you'll need to do this. The grains will end up breaking apart & coagulate after a couple of minutes of churning. This is visible to the naked eye. Remove from the heat and set aside to cool in the pot until it's safe to handle using your hands, approximately 15 minutes. If desired, add the lemon zest as well as fresh parsley.

• Shape into four tennis-ball-sized balls using moist hands. Place on a platter or a baking sheet. Flatten into a 1 to 1 1/2 inch thick pancake (approximately 3-4 inches wide) using moist hands, flattening any fissures on the borders and making them smooth and tidy. It's crucial to have wet hands.

• Refrigerate for 15 minutes to let the flavors meld. The quinoa cakes would become even more robust as they cool. (If you make these ahead of time, gently oil them, wrap them, and keep them in the fridge for 3-4 days.)

• In a well-oiled saucepan, gently roast the Quinoa Cakes over the moderate flame (flipping with a thin metal spoon). You may pan-sear them without covering them or dip them in rice flour or gluten-free Panko for an additional crispy crust. Just keep an eye on them and don't touch them until they've developed a nice crust before rotating. They will gradually detach themselves from the skillet as the crust develops.

- You can, however, bake them till heated through in a toaster (directly on the pan) or in a 400F oven for approximately 20 min, but the pan crust gives them the best consistency.

- Garnish with the fresh (tomato chickpea) relish, then distribute among plates. Any leftover dressing should be spooned over and all around the cakes.

- If desired, top with shredded goat cheese or a vinaigrette glaze.

## 48. RAMEN WITH SHIITAKE BROTH

Serving: 4

Preparation time: 1 hr.

Nutritional values: Calories-408kcal|Carbs-59g|Protein-14g|Fat-13g

## Ingredients

- 1 large, sliced onion
- 2 garlic cloves, crushed
- 1–2 tbsp. extra virgin olive oil
- 4 c. vegetable stock
- four cups of water
- 1/2 cup of dried Shiitake Mushrooms, diced
- 1 sheet of seaweed (Kombu)
- Mirin, 1/8 cup
- 1–2 tbsp. miso paste (white)
- salt and pepper to taste
- To make it spicy, add sriracha or hot chili oil to taste.

For ramen

- Ramen Noodles, 6–8 oz.
- Cubed Crispy Tofu, 8 oz.

## Directions

- If you're going to add roasted vegetables, start then. Mix bite-size chunks with some olive oil, salt, as well as pepper, then put on a parchment-lined baking sheet & roast until fork done, about 40 minutes.

To prepare the broth

- Fry the diced onion in one tbsp. oil over moderate flame until soft, approximately 3 minutes. Reduce the heat to moderate, add the crushed garlic cloves, and sauté the onions unless they are a rich golden brown color. Combine the vegetable stock, water, dry shiitakes, a strip of kombu (rinsed), plus mirin in a large mixing bowl. Bring to a boil, then reduce to low heat.

- Extract the Kombu after 25-30 minutes of simmering uncovered over medium heat. Stir the miso and season with salt and pepper to perfection. To taste, adjust the salt. Keep it warm. If this lowers too much, it may turn salty; just add a splash of water to taste.

- While the soup is cooking, prepare the ramen noodles as per package instructions in a saucepan of boiling water. Drain. To preserve it apart, stir with sesame oil.

- Prepare the remaining vegetables and garnishes. Steam or fry bok choy / fresh spinach until barely tender. Whether using mushrooms, sauté till cooked in a little oil, sprinkling with salt and black pepper. For the finest texture, combine fresh and cooked vegetables.

To assemble the ramen bowls

- Toss boiled noodles, crispy tofu, and any other vegetables you want into bowls. Overtop, pour the delicious Shiitake broth. Serve with a sprinkle of sesame oil as well as sriracha on top. Add onions and sesame seeds to the top.

- Serve right away.

## 49. FARMER'S MARKET FRIED RICE

Serving: 4

Preparation time: 40 min

Nutritional values: Calories-453kcal|Carbs-52g|Protein-16g|Fat-21g

### Ingredients

- Tofu (8 oz.) (or 2 eggs, whisked)
- Coconut oil (approximately 4–5 tbsp.) (or peanut oil, extra virgin olive oil, or butter/ghee)
- 1 onion, chopped or 2 leeks (diced and washed)
- 3 rough diced garlic cloves
- 4 cups diced vegetables: carrots, cabbage, asparagus, kale, broccoli, etc.
- 1 cup of edamame or peas, shelled (frozen)
- 3 cups of rice, cooked, cold, and dry
- 3 tbsp. soy sauce (gluten-free) Amino acids in liquid form
- 1 tsp. toasted sesame oil
- Salt and black pepper as per taste-
- 1/4 tsp. toasted sesame oil for each
- 1/4 cup of scallions
- Furikake or roasted sesame seeds, 1–2 tsp.

### Directions

- Whisk the eggs or tofu in an extra-large cast-iron skillet with 2 tbsp. oil over moderate flame. If you're using tofu, make sure it's completely dry before breaking it up with the fork in the pan. Add a sprinkle of salt and black pepper to taste. Place on a wide platter and set aside.
- Add the oil in the same skillet over medium heat and sauté the leeks as well as onion. When the vegetables are soft, add the garlic and cook for 1-2 minutes. Reduce the heat to moderate and add the longer-cooking vegetables first, such as carrots & mushrooms, followed by the other vegetables, saving the greens, kale, or cabbage for last. Mix in the chilled edamame, then put the vegetables aside beside tofu.
- Pour enough oil into the pan to gently coat it. Pour in the rice and smooth it out evenly. Increase the heat to medium-high and cook for a few minutes, avoiding the temptation to stir continuously. Using a knife, flip the rice into large chunks and fry up both sides. Return the tofu (either egg) plus vegetables to the rice after it has reached the desired crispiness. To mix, give it a thorough stir. Toss in the soy sauce, oil, then season to taste with salt and pepper. Mix in the Hondashi a bit at a time if using. Adjust the soy sauce as well as sesame oil to taste and add more if desired.
- Garnish with fresh scallions & Furikake (toasted sesame seeds) in individual bowls.
- Fried rice may be kept in the fridge for up to four days and warmed on the burner or in the microwave.

## 50. BAKED SHEETPAN RATATOUILLE

Serving: 4-6

Preparation time: 1 hr. 15 min

Nutritional values: Calories-147kcal|Carbs-15g|Protein-2g|Fat-9g

### Ingredients

- 3 large eggplants or 3 Japanese eggplants
- 1 bell pepper (red or yellow)
- 2 tomatoes (medium)
- 2 summer squash or zucchini
- 1 medium onion
- 8–14 whole, scraped garlic cloves
- 2–3 tbsp. fresh herbs (thyme, rosemary, or a mix of both)

- A sprinkling of olive oil
- To taste, salt & black pepper
- A squirt of balsamic vinegar

For creamy polenta

- cornmeal, 1 cup
- 4 1/2 cup of stock or water
- 1 tbsp. butter or olive oil
- 1/2 cup shredded cheese ( your preference)
- To taste, salt and pepper

## Directions

- Preheat the oven to 400 degrees F and line two large sheet pans with parchment paper.
- Scrape eggplant using a potato peeler if desired – or just peel part of the skin in large strips. Keep the skin on if you want. Chop into bite-sized 1/2-inch-thick chunks. Bell peppers should be cut into 1/2-inch broad strips. Tomatoes should be cut into 3/4-inch slices. Cut the zucchini lengthwise and then into 1/2-inch-thick half-moon slices. Cut the onion half-moons into 1/4-1/2-inch-thick half-moons.
- Arrange the vegetables in a thin layer on the sheet pan. Add full (peeled) garlic cloves & seasonings.
- Mix with olive oil, using just enough to coat the vegetables. Season with a good pinch of salt & pepper. Toss thoroughly.
- Bake for twenty minutes in a hot oven, combine the vegetables, roast for another 20 minutes, and mix again. Reduce the heat to 300°F and continue to roast for another 10-20 minutes, or until the vegetables are soft and the edges are beginning to caramelize.
- Taste, season with salt and finish with a spritz of balsamic vinegar.
- Consume right away, or cool and chill (or freeze) until needed.

# 51. OAXACAN BOWL

Serving: 2

Preparation time: 40 min

Nutritional values: Calories-489kcal|Carbs-73g|Protein-16g|Fat-18g

## Ingredients

- Cumin (2 tsp.)
- 1 tsp. chipotle powder
- 1/2 tsp. kosher salt

Ingredients for the sheet pan

- 1/2 red onion slices (cut into 1/2 inch wedges)
- 1 medium sweet potato or yam, chopped into 3/4-inch chunks
- 8 half-cut baby bell peppers
- Pecans, 1/2 cup
- Maple syrup (two tsp.)
- 1 can of seasoned black beans (Cuban / Mexican style) or plain black beans, 15-16 oz.

For the quick cabbage slaw

- 1/4 cup grated red cabbage
- 1 tbsp. extra virgin olive oil
- 1/4 cup cilantro, scallions, or both, diced
- 1 tsp. coriander, chopped
- 1/8 tsp. salt (kosher)
- Lime juice, 1 tbsp.

## Directions

- Preheat the oven to 400 degrees Fahrenheit.
- In a small bowl, combine cumin, chipotle, as well as salt.
- On a parchment-lined baking tray, place

- Preheat the oven to 200°F and bake for 20-30 minutes, stirring halfway through.

- Nuts: Mix the nuts with 2 tsp. Maple syrup and 1 tsp. of the seasoning mix in a separate parchment-lined baking sheet. Put in the oven for 5 to 6 min, stir, & bake for another 2-3 minutes until gently browned. (It's worth noting that they burn quickly.) Giving the nuts a short toss as you take them out to soften them up & "fluffen" them, so they are easier to remove after they cool.

- Make the slaw while heating the spiced beans in a medium saucepan on the stove. Mix the cabbage with the other components in a separate bowl after finely chopping or shredding it. Adjust the lime and salt to taste.

- Cut the avocado into slices.

- Assemble the dishes after the vegetables are fork-tender. Using 2-3 dishes, distribute the beans. Place all of the vegetables on top of the beans, then cover with slaw & avocado.

- If desired, top with Chipotle Mayo (vegan-friendly) or Vegan Avocado Sauce, as well as sour cream & hot sauce.

## 52. ORECCHIETTE WITH CREAMY CARROT MISO SAUCE

Serving: 3-4

Preparation time: 45 min

Nutritional values: Calories-393kcal|Carbs-59g|Protein-11g|Fat-12g

### Ingredients

- 8–10 oz. Orecchiette pasta, boiled as per package instructions in salted water.

For miso carrot sauce

- 2 shallots (or 1/2 onion) roughly diced
- 4–6 cloves garlic, roughly diced
- 2 tbsp. extra virgin olive oil
- 2 heaped cups of finely chopped carrots (3 midsized carrots)
- 2 c. water
- 1/4 cup of cashews, raw
- Salt (1/4 tsp.)
- 1/4 tsp. of pepper
- 3 tbsp. Miso Paste (White)

### Directions

To prepare the pasta

- Bring 6 to 8 cups of salted water to a boil for the pasta, then cook as per package instructions.

To prepare the sauce

- In a medium saucepan, add the oil over moderate flame. Cook, often tossing, until the shallot and garlic are aromatic and golden, approximately 5 minutes. Bring the carrots, diced cashews, water, salt, & pepper to a simmer. Cover, reduce heat to low, and cook for 15 minutes, or unless carrots are fork-tender. Allow it cool for 5 to 10 min after adding the 3 tbsp of miso (it does not need to be completely dissolved).

- In a high-powered blender, combine all of the ingredients and cover firmly with a kitchen towel. Pulse on the lowest speed, slowly increasing the speed, until completely incorporated, creamy, as well as silky smooth, approximately 1-1 1/2 minutes. Take some time and make sure it's smooth.

- Rinse the pasta, then ladle the sauce over it, reheating it slightly if necessary. Taste & adjust the salt as needed.

- Distribute among dishes, cover with toasted bread crumbs, and drizzle with the delicious Carrot Top Gremolata if desired.

# 53. BLACK PEPPER TOFU WITH BOK CHOY

Serving: 2

Preparation time: 30 min

Nutritional values: Calories-463kcal|Carbs-37g|Protein-24g|Fat-24g

## Ingredients

- 8–12 oz. firm tofu wiped dry and chunks of 1 inch
- 2 tbsp. oil for wok
- A hefty pinch of salt (5 fingers)
- 1 tsp. peppercorns, freshly cracked
- 1 shallot, fat, chopped
- 4 garlic cloves, roughly diced
- 6 oz. (approximately 4) baby bok choy, cut into quarters crosswise

For the sauce

- 2 tbsp. soy sauce (optional)
- 2 tbsp. Shaoxing Rice Wine (Chinese Cooking Wine) or dry white wine, pale sherry, or rice wine
- Water, 2 tbsp.
- 1 tsp. sugar (brown)
- 1/2 tsp. peppercorns, freshly cracked
- 1 tsp. paste of chili (optional)

## Directions

- Tofu should be cut into chunks and blotted dry using paper towels, gently pushing down.
- To prepare the wok sauce, combine all of the components in a small bowl and whisk until all sugar has dissolved. Put it near the stove.
- Prepare the bok choy, shallots, & garlic.
- Using a light layer of corn starch, cover the tofu
- Add the oil in a wok / wide cast iron pan over medium-high heat, then stir in the salt & cracked peppercorns until aromatic, approximately one minute.
- Cook the tofu in the flavored oil until brown and crispy on both sides, lowering the heat if necessary. It will take approximately 5-6 minutes.
- Wipe clean the pan and set the crunchy tofu away on a napkin dish.
- Over moderate flame, add additional tsp. or two of oil, along with the shallots, garlic, as well as bok choy. Stir constantly for 3-4 minutes, or until bok choy starts to wilt & shallots become yellow. It'll smell fantastic. Pour the wok sauce into the pan, being sure to scrape off any sugar that has collected in the bowl.
- Cook for a few minutes or until the bok choy is barely soft.
- Stir the tofu, bok choy, as well as sauce back into the skillet at the very end. If you cook it much longer, the wonderful crispiness will be lost! Check for salt & heat, and adjust as needed.
- Instantly serve, dividing among two bowls.

# 54. INSTANT POT MUJADRA

Serving: 5

Preparation time: 35 min

Nutritional values: Calories-429kcal|Carbs-63g|Protein-14g|Fat-14g

## Ingredients

- 1 cup of lentils, medium brown
- 1 1/2 tbsp. extra virgin olive oil
- 2–3 finely chopped fat shallots (one red onion)
- 4 garlic cloves, coarsely sliced
- Cumin (2 tsp.)

- 1 tsp. coriander powder
- 1 tsp. allspice powder
- 1/2 tsp. of cinnamon
- 1/2 tsp. turmeric, if desired
- 1/4 tsp. ginger powder
- 1 1/2 tsp. salt (kosher)
- 1 tsp. dried parsley or mint
- The zest of one tiny lemon
- 3 cup (changed from 3 1/2 cup) water
- 1 cup washed & drained brown basmati rice

## Directions

- Cover a bowl halfway with hot distilled water and immerse lentils until ready to use in the instant pot.

- Set the Instant Pot to Fry mode. Shallots should be cooked for 4-5 min in the oil, stirring continuously, until soft, aromatic, and slightly caramelized. Remove half of the mixture and set it aside for the topping. Fry the garlic for 1-2 minutes or until aromatic. Combine all of the seasonings, salt, lemon zest, as well as water in a large mixing bowl. Stir.

- Strain the lentils & rinse the rice before adding them to the pot. Give everything a good swirl.

- Lock the instant pot & set the timer for 11 min on high pressure. Give a minimum of 10 min for natural release.

- In the meanwhile, prepare any desired garnishes.

- To serve, muss the Mujadara with a spatula lightly. Toss tomatoes, avocado, caramelized shallots, sprouts, a dollop of yogurt or zhoug yogurt, either tahini sauce, plus fresh parsley or mint in separate dishes.

- Serve with additional seasonal vegetables if desired.

# 55. INSTANT POT LENTIL CURRY

Serving: 6

Preparation time: 30 min

Nutritional values: Calories-312kcal|Carbs-29g|Protein-10g|Fat-18g

## Ingredients

- 1-2 tbsp. coconut oil (or ghee)
- 1 chopped onion
- 6 coarsely diced garlic cloves (3-4 tbsp.)
- 2 tbsps. coarsely sliced ginger root
- 2 cups of chopped carrots
- 1 tbsp. cumin powder
- 2 tsp. coriander powder
- Salt (two tsp.)
- 1 1/2 tsp. turmeric powder (or 1 tbsp. freshly grated)
- Paprika, 1 tsp.
- 2 tsp. fenugreek leaves, dried
- 1 tsp. garam masala (garam masala)
- Nutmeg (1/2 tsp.)
- 1/4-3/4 tsp. cayenne pepper (or chili flakes) more to flavor
- 1 tbsp. paste of tomato
- 2 c. water
- 1 cup of lentils, brown
- 13.5 oz. coconut milk can

## Directions

- Add 1 tsp. black mustard seeds & 1 tsp. fennel seeds to enhance the flavor.

- Configure the Instant Pot to Fry mode, add the oil, & sauté the onion for 3 minutes, or until aromatic. Fry the garlic, ginger, and carrots for another 3 minutes, stirring occasionally. Stir in the remaining spices, salt, as well as tomato paste for 1 minute. Scrounge up any browned pieces from the base of the pan with the water.

- Incorporate the brown lentils, mix well, as well as pressure cook for ten minutes on medium.
- Add the coconut milk and mix well.
- You may also add additional vegetables at this stage, such as peas, cauliflower, or even a bunch of spinach to wilt if desired.
- Taste for salt, and season with more if required (particularly if using a lot of vegetables), as well as additional Garam Masala or chili flakes to taste.
- As it cools, the curry will thicken somewhat.
- Eat with homemade naan or over a mound of baby spinach and basmati rice.
- Put a small pan over medium-low heat to prepare the turmeric coconut chips. Top with 1/2 tsp. powdered turmeric and 1/4 cup of coconut flakes. Gently fry for a few minutes, until aromatic and gently toasted, stirring continuously. Turn the heat off. Don't walk away from them since they're very susceptible to burn.

## 56. VEGGIE LO MEIN

Serving: 2

Preparation time: 30 min

Nutritional values: Calories-258kcal|Carbs-35g|Protein-4g|Fat-12g

### Ingredients

- 4-5 oz. lo mein noodles, dry

For the sauce (Lo Mein)

- Soy sauce, 3 tbsp.
- 2 tbsp. cooking wine (Chinese) (or mirin, or 1 1/2 tbsp. water plus 1/2 tsp. rice vinegar plus 1/2 tsp. honey)
- 1 tbsp. sauce (oyster)
- 2 tsp. sesame seed oil
- 1 tsp. maple syrup, honey, or sugar
- 1/4 tsp. of liquid smoke
- White pepper, 1/8 tsp.
- Sriracha, 1/2–1 tsp. (or chili paste)

For stir-fried lo mein

- 2 tbsp. wok oil, peanut butter, or coconut oil
- 1/2 coarsely chopped onion
- 2 cups of mushrooms, chopped
- 3 rough diced garlic cloves
- 1 tsp. ginger (finely chopped)
- 1/2 coarsely chopped red bell pepper
- 1 cup carrots, cut into matchsticks
- 1 cup of cabbage, shredded
- 1 cup of peas (snow peas)

### Directions

- Bring a pot of water to a simmer, then boil the noodles as per the package instructions.
- In a medium mixing bowl, combine the components for the Lo Mein Sauce.
- Prepare any and all vegetables and keep them close to the burner.
- Add the oil in a wok or a wide pan over moderate flame. Sauté the onions as well as mushrooms for 3-4 minutes while constantly stirring. Reduce the heat to moderate and incorporate the garlic & ginger, cooking for 2 minutes. Stir the bell pepper, chopped carrots, cabbage, & snow peas, as well as cook, often stirring, for 3-4 minutes, or until soft but still crisp.
- Stir in the noodles and stir several times to fully integrate them.
- Pour the sauce (Lo Mein) as well as continue to mix and toss for two min. If it becomes too dry, add a dash of water to soften it up.

- Serve in two dishes with green onion on top.

# 57. VEGAN TLAYUDAS

Serving: 4

Preparation time: 40 min

Nutritional values: Calories-406kcal|Carbs-46g|Protein-10g|Fat-22g

## Ingredients

- 4 8-10 inch wide whole-grain tortillas (or gluten-free tortillas)

For cabbage slow

- 1/2 head of cabbage, grated (14–16 oz.)
- 1 cup of carrots, grated
- 4 coarsely chopped radishes
- 1/4 cup finely chopped red onion - pickled onions / pickled shallots may be substituted.
- 3/4 tsp. salt, plus more seasoning
- 1/2 diced English cucumbers
- 1 tbsp. coarsely chopped jalapeño
- 1/4–1/2 cup chopped scallions
- 1/4–1/2 cup diced cilantro
- 2 tbsp. extra virgin olive oil
- 3 tbsp. lime juice, + a tiny bit of zest

For cilantro-avocado sauce

- 1 avocado (moderate) (perfectly ripe)
- 4–6 pieces of jalapeno
- 1 clove of garlic
- 1/4-1/2 cup of cilantro (handful)
- 2 tbsp. extra virgin olive oil
- Lime juice (two tbsp.)
- Water, 4 tbsp.
- 1/2 tsp. of salt

## Directions

- Preheat the oven to 275 degrees Fahrenheit.

- Roast tortillas on oven grates (no sheet pan required) until crisp, approximately 20 minutes. This is crucial: they must be crisp and dry, not stretchy. You may prepare them ahead of time.

- Toss the cabbage, chopped carrots, radish, & onion with the salt in a large mixing bowl. (At first, this may seem to be a lot, but it will discharge liquid and diminish.)

- Combine the cucumber, diced jalapeno, diced scallions, and cilantro in a mixing bowl. Toss thoroughly, then drizzle with olive oil (extra virgin) and lime juice, along with a pinch of zest. Allow to cool on the counter, or prepare ahead of time and store in the refrigerator.

- If you're preparing the avocado sauce, do it right now by combining all of the ingredients in a stick blender and mixing until creamy. Taste & adjust the salt as well as spice level as required, using more jalapeno if necessary. Place in a mixing bowl.

- While ready to serve, simmer the refried beans with 1/4-1/2 cup of water (to soften them) & sprinkle to taste with a bit of salt, cumin, as well as coriander.

- Cook the chicken or chorizo immediately, and switch on the broiler if you're using cheese.

- To make the tortilla, gently smear some beans on it. You may either add chicken as well as cheese (or let it melt) at this stage or leave it out to make it vegan. A substantial mound of coleslaw should be placed on top of the heated base. Spread avocado sauce (or diced avocado) as well as Chipotle Mayo over the top.

- Add cilantro sprigs (diced), hot sauce, lime slices, pickled onions, or shallots as garnish. Although the beans are still warm as well as the tortillas are crisp, serve instantly (with knife & fork).

- Enjoy.

# 58. SZECHUAN TOFU & VEGGIES

Serving: 2

Preparation time: 30 min

Nutritional values: Calories-307kcal|Carbs-24g|Protein-14g|Fat-20g

## Ingredients

- 8–12 oz. tofu, diced & patted dry
- 2 tbsp. peanut oil or other high-heat oil
- A sprinkle of salt and pepper
- 1/2 cup onion, finely diced
- 4 oz. mushrooms, diced (optional)
- 2 cups of cabbage, chopped
- 1 cup of carrots, grated or matchsticks
- 1/2 coarsely chopped red bell pepper
- 1 cup of green beans, asparagus, or snap peas
- Optional: 6-8 tiny dried red Arbol / Chinese chilies
- 1/4 cup of Szechuan sauce, plus more to flavor

## Directions

- In a saucepan, heat the oil. Season the oil with salt and black pepper to taste. Stir the flavored oil throughout until it is evenly distributed. Sear the tofu on a minimum of two sides until brown and crispy. Place aside.
- Put some more oil, onion, as well as mushrooms into the same skillet and cook over medium-high heat, stirring continuously, until soft, approximately 3 minutes. Reduce heat to medium and incorporate vegetables, along with the dried red chills if using, and sauté, tossing and turning for 3-5 minutes, until just cooked or al dente. Tender yet vibrant, with a touch of crispness!
- Begin with a 1/4 cup of Szechuan sauce, then apply more to taste. If you're making several batches, you'll need to adjust the sauce appropriately. Cook for 2 minutes, or until the sauce has thickened somewhat. Just before serving, throw in the crunchy tofu to heat it up.
- Divide the mixture among the bowls. Garnish with sesame seeds as well as onions. To increase the heat, add chili flakes.
- Serve it plain, over rice, or over noodles.

# 59. MIDDLE EASTERN SALAD TACOS

Serving: 3

Preparation time: 20 min

Nutritional values: Calories-405kcal|Carbs-56g|Protein-13g|Fat-15g

## Ingredients

- 2 tsp. extra virgin olive oil
- 1 can of washed & drained chickpeas
- 1 tsp. sumac powder
- 1 tsp. cumin powder
- 1/4–1/2 tsp. of salt
- Sesame seeds, 1 tsp.
- 1/2 cup of hummus (also known as baba ganoush or tahini sauce) (not paste)
- 6 × 6 inches warmed or gently browned tortillas
- Salad with Lemon
- Arugula in a good amount
- 1 chopped tomato
- 2 chopped Turkish cucumbers
- 1–2 tbsp. extra virgin olive oil
- Lemon juice, 1–2 tbsp.
- 1 tsp. coriander powder

- 1/4 tsp. salt, plus more to taste

### Directions

- In a wide skillet, heat the oil over a moderate flame. Add chickpeas, spices, plus salt to taste. Warm thoroughly, stirring occasionally. Stir the sesame seeds just before serving. Turn off the heat.

- In a large mixing bowl, combine the salad ingredients. Heat the tortillas gently until they are warm and malleable.

- On a heated tortilla, apply hummus or baba ganoush. Garnish with a generous pile of salad and heated chickpeas. Garnish with onions and herbs.

## 60. ROASTED PORTOBELLO STEAKS WITH WALNUT COFFEE SAUCE

Serving: 4

Preparation time: 35 min

Nutritional values: Calories-408kcal|Carbs-16g|Protein-8g|Fat-37g

### Ingredients

- 4 portobello mushrooms, extremely large
- 2 tbsp. extra virgin olive oil
- 1 tbsp. balsamic vinegar
- A sprinkle of salt and pepper

For the coffee sauce with walnuts

- 3 tbsp. extra virgin olive oil
- 2 large shallots, coarsely chopped (about 3/4–1 cup)
- 4 roughly diced garlic cloves
- Walnuts, 1 cup (raw)
- 1/4 cup of black coffee (cold or decaffeinated is OK) or broth
- 1/2 tsp. of salt
- 1/2 tsp. black pepper
- 1 tsp. of miso
- 1 tsp. balsamic vinegar

### Directions

- Preheat the oven to 400 degrees Fahrenheit.

- In a small container, combine the oil & vinegar and coat both sides of the Portobellos with it. Season with salt & pepper, then put on a parchment-lined baking sheet, gills downwards. Bake for 20 to 25 min, or until the potatoes are soft. Wrap in foil and set aside until prepared for use.

- Make the sauce whilst portobellos are roasting.

- In a wide saucepan, heat the oil over moderate flame. Cook, often turning, until the shallots, as well as garlic, are aromatic and soft, approximately 4-5 minutes. Toss in the walnuts for two min. Scrape off any brown pieces before adding the coffee. Pour everything into a blender, along with the salt, pepper, paste of miso, and balsamic vinegar, and mix until ultra-smooth. Return the sauce to the pan and reheat gently just before serving.

- Once the portobellos are ready, chop them and put them on a serving platter with the Coffee Walnut sauce, or dish them separately with (roasted) garlic mashed potatoes

- For added color, garnish with a bunch of thyme as well as pomegranate seeds. Season with a pinch of salt and freshly crushed pepper. If you really like (truffle) oil, a little trickle is usually a great way to up the odds.

## 61. ZUCCHANOUSH

Serving: 7

Preparation time: 15 min

Nutritional values: Calories-125kcal|Carbs-4g|Protein-3g|Fat-11g

### Ingredients

- 1 pound (approximately 3) medium zucchini, cut into quarters lengthwise
- 3 tbsp. extra virgin olive oil halved
- Salt & pepper, kosher
- 1 garlic clove
- Tahini (1/4 cup)
- 2 tablespoons freshly squeezed lemon juice
- 3 tablespoons mint leaves (distributed)
- 1 tablespoon roasted pine nuts

## Directions

- Preheat the grill to a moderate flame. Mix zucchini with 1 tbsp. oil & 1/2 tsp. salt & grill for 8 to 10 minutes, or until soft and uniformly browned.
- Add zucchini, garlic, tahini, juice (lemon), and 1 tbsp. mint to a mixer and pulse to incorporate. Drizzle in the leftover 2 tbsp. olive oil and blend on moderate speed until almost smooth, adjusting blender speed if required.
- Chop the remaining mint leaves. Serve the zucchini combination with mint & pine nuts on top.

## 62. CUCUMBER MELON SOUP

Serving: 4

Preparation time: 45 min

Nutritional values: Calories-75kcal|Carbs-18g|Protein-3g|Fat-0g

## Ingredients

- 1 pound English cucumbers, chopped up, with more for serving
- 1/2 medium honeydew melon (approximately 1 lb.), seeds and skin removed, sliced into pieces
- Half cup of flat-parsley leaves
- 3 tablespoons vinegar (red wine)
- 1 tablespoon lime juice
- 2 teaspoons sugar
- Salt & pepper, kosher
- Watercress, to be used as a garnish

## Directions

- Blend cucumbers (diced), melon, leaves of parsley, red wine vinegar, and juice of lime, sugar, & 1/2 tsp. salt in a processor until smooth.
- Chill for at least one hour or up to 24 hours. Serve with watercress, cucumber slices, as well as cracked pepper on top.

## 63. TOFU PAD THAI

Serving: 4

Preparation time: 35 min

Nutritional values: Calories-440kcal|Carbs-73g|Protein-16g|Fat-10g

## Ingredients

- 14 ounces drained extra-firm tofu
- 8 ounces rice noodles 2 tablespoons corn-starch
- 1/4 cup soy sauce (low sodium)
- Brown sugar, 2 tablespoons
- Sweet chili sauce, 2 teaspoons
- 1 lime juice, with lime wedges to serve
- 1 garlic clove, shredded
- 1 tablespoon olive oil
- 1 diced red pepper
- 2 c. sprouted mung beans
- 2 coarsely chopped scallions
- 1/4 cup of peanuts, diced

## Directions

- Cut tofu into 1/2-inch slices. Put among sheets of paper towels on prepared baking sheet; cover with 2nd sheet and weight down with cast iron pan for 10 minutes. Cut into chunks and mix with corn-starch in a container.

- Next, cook the noodles according to package instructions and drain them after rinsing with cool water.

- Mix soy sauce, sugar, chili sauce, juice of the lime, and garlic in a mixing bowl; put aside.

- In a wide non-stick skillet, add 1 tbsp. oil over moderate flame. Cook, occasionally stirring, until the pepper is soft, about 4 to 5 min. Remove the pan from the heat. Cook, occasionally turning, until lightly browned, about 4 - 5 minutes. Toss in the noodles as well as a sauce to mix. Cook for 2 minutes after adding the pepper, sprouts, & scallions.

## 64. SPICED FRESH TOMATO SOUP WITH SWEET & HERBY PITAS

Serving: 4

Preparation time: 25 min

Nutritional values: Calories-325kcal|Carbs-43g|Protein-6g|Fat-16g

### Ingredients

For soup

- 2 tablespoons of olive oil
- 1 onion, medium
- 1 red pepper, medium (both chopped)
- Half teaspoon of salt
- 2 garlic cloves
- 1 jalapeno pepper
- 1 ginger chunk, 1 inch
- 2 teaspoon coriander powder
- 1 teaspoon cumin powder
- 2 1/2 pounds of tomatoes (roughly chopped)
- 2 1/2 cups of water
- 2 pitas (pocket-free)

Topping

- Brown sugar, 1 tablespoon
- 2 tablespoons olive oil/butter
- 2 tablespoons unsweetened coconut, coarsely shredded
- 2 tablespoons cilantro

### Directions

- To make the soup, follow these steps: Preheat a large Dutch oven to moderate. Heat the oil, then the onion, diced red pepper, & salt, and simmer, covered, for 8 - 10 min, until the onion is soft.

- Next, grate the garlic, jalapeno, & ginger thinly. Cook for 1 minute, stirring constantly. Cook for 1 minute after adding the crushed coriander & cumin.

- Increase the heat to high and cook, partly covered, for 10 minutes. Heat 2 pocket-less pitas, whereas the tomatoes are simmering.

- Puree the soup in sections using an electric mixer (or a regular blender).

- To prepare the topping, mix brown sugar, butter, roughly chopped unsweetened coconut, & cilantro in a mixing dish. Pour the overheated mixture pitas, then carve and serve with the soup.

## 65. BBQ CHICKPEA & CAULIFLOWER FLATBREADS WITH AVOCADO MASH

Serving: 4

Preparation time: 15 min

Nutritional values: Calories-500kcal|Carbs-65g|Protein-11g|Fat-25g

## Ingredients

- Tiny cauliflower florets (12 oz.)
- Extra-virgin olive oil, 1 tablespoon
- Salt

For BBQ, chickpea "nuts."

- 2 avocados, ripe
- Lemon juice, 2 tablespoons.
- 4 toasted flatbreads / pocket-less pitas
- 2 tablespoons salted roasted pepitas
- To serve, hot sauce

## Directions

- Mix cauliflower with extra virgin olive oil & 1/4 tsp. salt on a large prepared baking sheet; roast for twenty-five minutes with 1/4 recipe BBQ Chickpea "Nuts" in a 425°F oven.

- Mash avocados with juice of a lemon and a sprinkle of salt; put over flatbreads. Garnish with roasted cauliflower, chickpeas, as well as pepitas. Serve with a squirt of hot sauce on top.

## 66. TAHINI LEMON QUINOA WITH ASPARAGUS RIBBONS

Serving: 4

Preparation time: 45 min

Nutritional values: Calories-525kcal|Carbs-64g|Protein-20g|Fat-24g

## Ingredients

- 1 washed 15-ounce can of chickpeas
- 1 lemon, zest & juice
- Salt, kosher
- Pepper
- 1 cup of quinoa
- Tahini (1/2 cup)
- Lime juice, 1/4 cup
- 1 tablespoon honey/agave nectar
- 1 cup of fresh mint leaves, packaged
- 1 pound of thick asparagus
- 1/4 cup of sliced shelled pistachios

## Directions

- Mix chickpeas, lemon zest and juice, and a sprinkle of salt and pepper in a mixing bowl. Drain after 20 minutes of chilling or overnight in the refrigerator.

- Next, cook the quinoa according to the package instructions, seasoning with a sprinkle of salt.

- Mash tahini, juice of a lime, honey, diced mint, 1/2 cup of water, and 1/4 tsp. salt in a food processor or blender, adding more water if necessary; set aside.

- Chop asparagus into ribbons using a potato peeler, peeling from the woody end to the tip. Mix prepared quinoa, asparagus ribbons, as well as marinated chickpeas in a mixing bowl. Spritz with tahini sauce and top with pistachios.

## 67. ROASTED VEGGIES AND TEMPEH BOWL

Serving: 1

Preparation time: 10 min

Nutritional values: Calories-245kcal|Carbs-20g|Protein-14g|Fat-12g

## Ingredients

- 1 cup of spinach (baby)
- 1/2 cup of red cabbage, chopped
- 1 cup of quinoa
- 1 cup of roasted vegetables (assorted)
- 1 roasted tempeh piece

- 2 tablespoons cilantro, diced
- 1/4 teaspoon sesame oil, roasted
- Radishes, chopped
- Slice of lime

## Directions

- Cover the bowl with spinach (baby), grated red cabbage, prepared quinoa, plus roasted vegetables.
- Pour with toasted (sesame) oil and sprinkle with cooked tempeh & diced cilantro.
- Microwave for a few minutes.
- Serve with chopped radishes as well as a lime slice on the side.

## 68. CRISPY POTATOES WITH VEGAN NACHO SAUCE

Serving: 4

Preparation time: 45 min

Nutritional values: Calories-380kcal|Carbs-47g|Protein-10g|Fat-18g

## Ingredients

- 2 lb. halved mixed baby potatoes
- 3 tablespoons of canola oil
- 1 cup of unsalted, raw cashews, steeped & drained
- Lemon juice, 3 tablespoons
- Half teaspoon of chili powder
- Cumin powder (1/2 teaspoon)
- Half teaspoon of sweet paprika
- Half teaspoon of garlic powder
- 1 teaspoon coarse salt
- 1/4 cup of nutritional yeast
- 1/2 seeded & diced jalapeno chile

## Directions

- Preheat the oven at 450 degrees Fahrenheit. Combine the potatoes, oil, 1/2 tsp. salt, & 1/4 tsp. pepper in a mixing bowl. Distribute potatoes uniformly on a lined baking sheet and roast for 30 minutes, turning once, until brown and crispy.
- Next, in a processor with 1 cup of water, blend cashews, juice of lemon, chili powder, ground cumin, powder of paprika, garlic powder, salt (sea), nutritional yeast, & jalapeño until smooth. Simmer on medium-low for 5 minutes, or until heated, stirring periodically, in a 2-quart pot. Transfer to a serving dish and top with roasted potatoes.

## 69. ASIAN SESAME ZUCCHINI NOODLES

Serving: 4

Preparation time: 15 min

Nutritional values: Calories-85kcal|Carbs-12g|Protein-2g|Fat-4g

## Ingredients

- 1/4 cup cilantro, coarsely diced, packaged
- 3 tablespoons rice vinegar (seasoned)
- 1 tablespoon sesame oil that has been roasted
- 2 garlic cloves, smashed with a press
- 2 teaspoons red pepper flakes
- 2 teaspoons sugar
- 3 large spiralized zucchini

## Directions

- Combine cilantro, vinegar, sesame oil, crushed garlic, red pepper, sugar, & 1/2 tsp. salt in a large mixing bowl.
- Toss in the zucchini until everything is thoroughly mixed. Serve right away.

# 70. CREAMY VEGAN LINGUINE WITH MILD MUSHROOMS

Serving: 6

Preparation time: 20 min

Nutritional values: Calories-430kcal|Carbs-62g|Protein-15g|Fat-15g

## Ingredients

- Linguine or fettuccine, 1 pound
- 6 tablespoons extra virgin olive oil
- 12 oz. thinly chopped assorted mushrooms
- 3 garlic cloves, coarsely diced
- 1/4 cup of nutritional yeast
- 2 finely diced green onions

## Directions

- Cook the linguine according to the package directions, reserving 3/4 cup of the noodle boiling water before draining. Return the linguine to the saucepan once it has been drained.

- Next, add the oil in a 12-inch skillet over medium-high heat. Stir in the mushrooms & garlic for 5 minutes, or until the mushrooms are golden and soft. Add nutritional yeast, leftover cooking water, 1/2 tsp. salt, and 3/4 tsp. Roughly crushed pepper to the saucepan with the cooked, drained linguine. Whirl until everything is thoroughly mixed. Serve with green onions as a garnish.

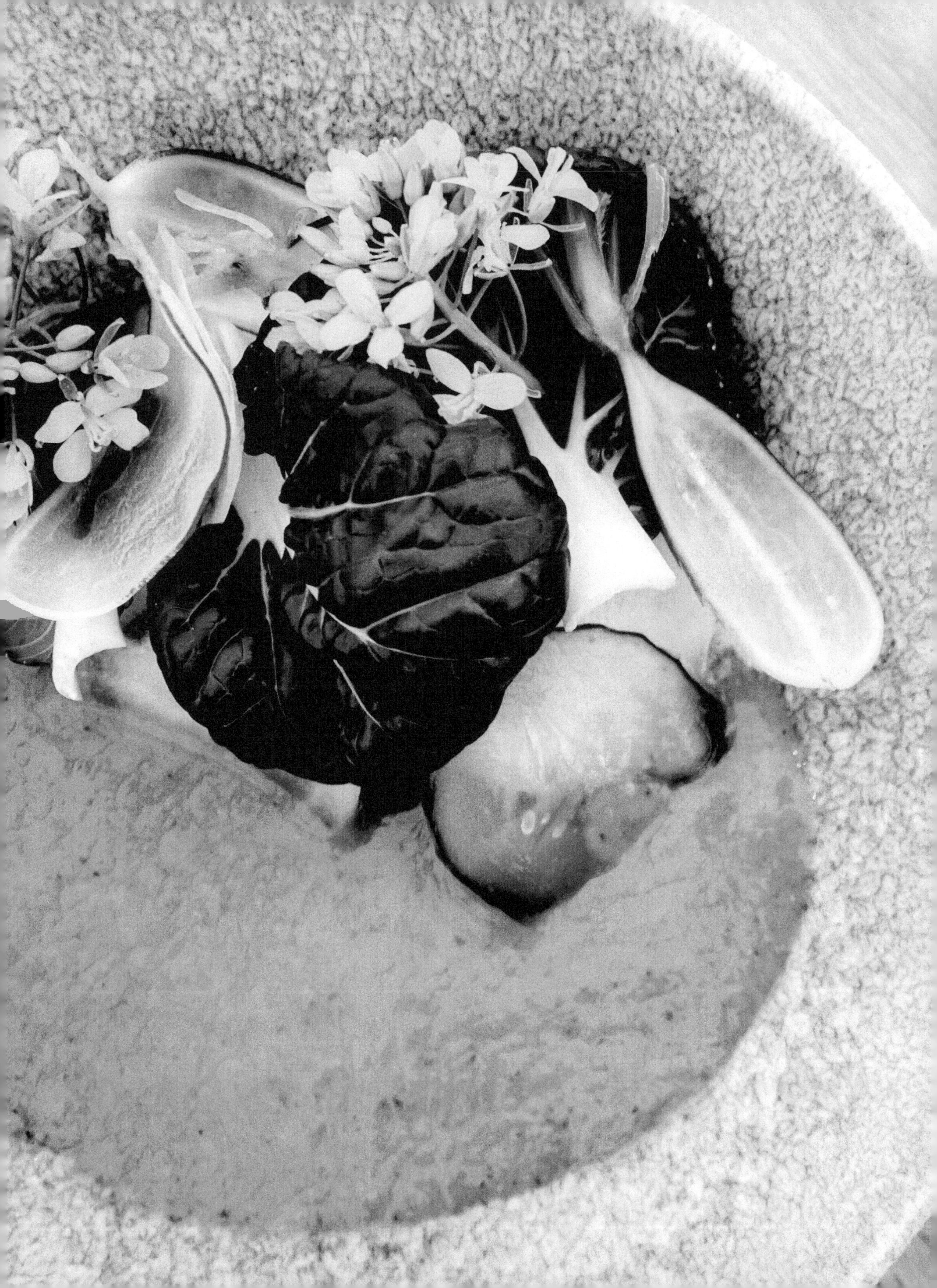

# CONCLUSION

Paleo & vegan diets have indeed been paired to create the ideal healthy lifestyle, completely changing people's eating habits. This "pegan" cookbook is the ideal combination of two popular diets for people seeking complete, fresh, and sustainable cuisine rich in healthy fats & vitamins. This vegan, plant-based diet will allow you to eat all of your favorite foods while staying active and living a healthier approach.

Despite the fact that veggies are inherently low in carbohydrates, most of us consume considerably too many of them. Getting adequate protein is one of the most difficult challenges individuals encounter while following a vegetarian or vegan diet.

Pegan refers to "Paleo" & "Vegan," and it's a cross between the two popular diets that aim to lose weight without losing any of the advantages. That implies that followers are free to consume quite so much fruit as they like, but sweets like cane sugar & honey should be avoided. Similarly, followers are allowed to consume wine as well as other alcoholic drinks in moderation.

Followers, on the other hand, are not allowed to eat dairy products or processed meals. This is due to the fact that such foods are rich in carbohydrates and also include a lot of harmful fats such as saturated fats. Instead, adherents must consume as much organic meat and veggies as possible while avoiding junk food.

The Pegan diet varies from the paleo & vegan diets in that adherents may get protein from any source. So, although most paleo dieters eat bacon or chicken, if you wish to live a Pegan lifestyle, you may eat beef or even other red meats. The Pegan diet offers many health advantages. First and foremost, followers should anticipate losing weight as a result of their participation. Because the diet enables adherents to get tasty, nutritious fats from grass-fed meats & omega-3 fatty acids from fish, the diet is popular.

However, it is not just about losing weight; it is also about boosting general health. This is because adherents are urged not to consume processed meals or milk products, which frequently include harmful components such as sugar & saturated fats.

The Pegan diet is an excellent method to avoid many of the illnesses that are caused by consuming animal-based foods and fats. Heart disease, arthritis, excessive cholesterol, cancer, and other conditions are among them. Of course, the things you consume have a role as well. On a Pegan diet, adherents are encouraged to consume a lot of vegetables since this is where most of the carbohydrates in a meat-based eating plan originate from. Protein, and also vitamins & minerals, must be consumed in sufficient amounts.

Apart from weight reduction and improved health, there are additional advantages of living a Pegan lifestyle. A better night's sleep, improved mental clarity, and other benefits are possible. It's important to consume a variety of meals to make sure you're getting all of the minerals and vitamins you need. Eat plenty of fruits, vegetables, nuts, seafood, and eggs. Meals rich in nutritious proteins, including chicken breast, eggs, and grass-fed beef, are also suggested.

There are a few foods that Pegan devotees should avoid while on the regimen. Refined or fast food, processed sugar, low-fat meals, as well as dairy products are all examples. The Pegan diet is simple to begin with, and does not cost a lot of money. You'll need to purchase fresh vegetables and prepared meats like chicken & grass-fed beef, but apart from that, you can prepare all of the meals at home.

Made in United States
North Haven, CT
05 January 2022